Bruce Sandison is well known for his regular contri-
butions to *The Scotsman* and *Trout and Salmon*. He
also broadcasts on Radio Scotland and has recently
made a second series of programmes entitled *Tales of
the Loch*.

The Trout Lochs of Scotland – a fisherman's guide
was his first book and it has rapidly established itself
as the definitive work on the subject. Bruce Sandison
lives in Caithness surrounded by his large family and
by the best trout fishing in Scotland.

THE
SPORTING GENTLEMAN'S
GENTLEMAN

THE
SPORTING GENTLEMAN'S
GENTLEMAN

Tales from Scottish gillies

BRUCE SANDISON

UNWIN HYMAN
London   Sydney

First published in Great Britain by Unwin Hyman,
an imprint of Unwin Hyman Limited, 1987

UNWIN HYMAN LIMITED
Denmark House, 37-39 Queen Elizabeth Street,
London SE1 2QB
and
40 Museum Street, London WC1A 1LU

Allen & Unwin Australia Pty Ltd
8 Napier Street, North Sydney, NSW 2060, Australia

Allen & Unwin New Zealand Ltd, with the Port Nicholson Press
60 Cambridge Terrace, New Zealand.

British Library Cataloguing in Publication Data

```
Sandison, Bruce
  The sporting gentleman's gentleman :
  tales and stories from Scottish gillies.
1. Gillies —— Scotland
I. Title
799              SH609
ISBN 0-04-440041-1
```

Printed in Great Britain by Thetford Press, Thetford, Norfolk

For Ann

My best companion and friend for
twenty-five years on loch, moor and hill.
With love, affection and thanks.

Contents

Illustrations

The illustrations which appear at every chapter opening page have been reproduced by kind permission of *Punch*. *The Field* kindly made available their picture archive from which several of the above photos were identified.

Acknowledgement

My thanks are due, in fullest measure, to all the folk who gave so freely of their time and experience during my research for this book. Without their kindness, courtesy and consideration it could never have been written. I am indebted to them all.

I hope that the results of our joint efforts will give pleasure. For errors, omissions and sins, I beg forgiveness. If I have offended some, I apologise; if I have forgotten others, then may I lose the very next salmon I hook.

To my friends, the estate factors, gillies, keepers and stalkers and to the Scottish Arts Council, who helped me on my way with a Travel and Research Award, a hundred thousand thanks. And if the reader obtains but half the pleasure from reading these pages that I have had from writing them, then I shall be content.

Bruce Sandison
Ruther House
Watten
Caithness

CHAPTER 1

Jimmy Wallace
and the frontier lands
of Twizel, Tweed and Till

On Friday, 9 September, 1513, King James IV of Scotland led his army into battle against an English force commanded by the Earl of Surrey. Within a few hours the King was dead and the peerage of Scotland slain, leaving leaderless soldiers to fight on until cut down where they stood.

Such was the carnage that was Flodden Field, and I never pass between Crookham and Cornhill on the road to the Border Bridge at Coldstream without thinking of that terrible Black Friday when:

> *Even so it was, from Flodden Ridge*
> *The Scots beheld the English host*
> *Leave Barmoor Wood, their evening post,*
> *And headfully watched them as they crossed*
> *The Till by Twizel Bridge.*

1

A simple granite cross marks the battle-field, and the inscription on it speaks more eloquently of that fateful day than any words of mine: 'To the Brave of Both Nations. 1513.'

I had come to Twizel that morning seeking not revenge, but the pleasure of the company of Jim Wallace, one of the best-known and most-respected gillies on Tweed and Till. In any case, most of Surrey's army were from south of the Trent and considered Northumbrians to be as like Scots as to make little difference.

But as I stood on Twizel Bridge, looking towards Jim's cottage, which stands on the banks of the fast-flowing river, thoughts of Border ballads and ancient fights came flooding back.

I was born and brought up in the old grey city of Edinburgh and educated at one of Scotland's oldest places of learning, The Royal High School. Instruction in history was very much Scottish orientated, and as a boy my mind was filled with stories and tales of Randolph and Douglas, Andrew Wood with his ships *Flower* and *Yellow Carvel*, Wallace and Bruce, and of the near-constant feuding with our English neighbours.

My heart flamed to the story of the midnight Battle of Otterburn in 1388 and the death of Earl James Douglas: 'When he was overthrown the press was great about him, so he could not relieve, for with an axe he had his death's wound. Then Sir John Sinclair demanded of the Earl how he did. "Right evil, cousin," quoth the Earl, "but thanked be God there have been but few of mine ancestors that hath died in their beds."'

To a young, impressionable mind, this was stirring stuff. Romantic notions of honour and bravery became firmly fixed, as did a deep distrust of anything and every-thing south of Tweed. History is better taught today. My own children have a far better grasp of our island's story than the narrow, parochial view instilled into me.

Apart from a brief step over the Border as a young lad,

2

my first real journey out of Scotland was not made until I was summoned by the Queen for military service, and even then it was like a great adventure into unknown territory.

That first brief step came a few years after the end of the Second World War, when youngsters were encouraged to 'help Scotland's harvest'. A recruiting caravan was set up near the National Gallery in Princes Street, Edinburgh, and my elder brother and I signed on for two weeks.

We were paid handsomely for our efforts, had a holiday in the country, and worked in the fields, stacking sheaves and lifting potatoes. Best of all, real girls were working with us. The second most enduring memory of that autumn was when we were bundled into the back of a lorry and taken over the Border Bridge into England.

I do not really know what I expected: certainly something completely different—strange, dangerous-looking folk, perhaps, ready to cut a young Scot's throat as quick as a wink. It was with a still-remembered sense of astonishment that I realised that folk to the south of Tweed were exactly the same as their neighbours to the north. Nevertheless, with a caution born out of years of indoctrination, I stayed close to my brother—just in case.

I turned from these thoughts on Twizel Bridge and walked down the path to Jim's cottage. Going round to the back-door, I was greeted by a tall, well-built man, red-faced and smiling. Jim Wallace is not much shorter than myself, and I am six-feet-four.

We went through to the sitting-room and I explained the object of my visit. A log fire was burning brightly in hearth, and a black Labrador ambled in to greet me. To ward off the effects of the November chill, we fortified ourselves with a dram and settled to talk.

Jim Wallace has spent all his life as a gamekeeper and gillie on Tweed and Till. He was head gillie on the Till for many years and, when asked to return to the Tweed, his father, then aged seventy-five, took over as head gillie.

Jim's father died at the age of ninety-nine, fit as a fiddle to the last.

Jim caught his first salmon as a boy of nine. He remembers it clearly: 'It was in Mill Pool on Whiteadder, on a trout rod—no salmon rods for us lads in those days. An old lade came out of the mill and the river had that sweet evening smell, with water churning through the pool. You just knew you were going to catch fish.

'As light faded, sure enough, there came this great tug. My heart stopped. I would have given a year's pocket-money to have seen that fish on the bank there and then; instead it took damn near an hour. My arms were aching by the time I got it landed.

'There aren't so many fish about these days, what with salmon disease and netting. My gentlemen have to be patient and work hard for a fish, and at times even that isn't enough. But if you know your river, as every good gillie should, where the salmon lie and when they're most likely to take, then your gentlemen shouldn't often go home empty-handed.

'Some gentlemen are very skilful, particularly the younger ones. But just because a man casts forty to fifty yards doesn't mean he is going to catch salmon. Some gentlemen who come here are hardly able to cast at all, but they catch fish with no bother—and very annoying it is for their more able companions.

'I remember two gentlemen who used to fish with me, Mr Robson and Mr Scott. Now Mr Scott was a hard worker and expert caster—up at the crack of dawn, always first on the river, always last to leave. He would cast away non-stop all day, begrudging even a few moments for lunch. If fish were not taking, he would try every fly in his box, and then come to me for more.

'Mr Robson was quite the opposite. He would have a yarn before starting, ask after the family, wander round the garden, as different from his friend as night is from day, and hardly able to put out a line beyond his nose.

'Mr Robson always gave his friend first choice of where to fish, and I remember one morning, when Mr Scott had been lashing away in the pool, Mr Robson quietly took three lovely salmon from the run. Nothing would satisfy Mr Scott other than that he should fish the run in the afternoon, so I took him over in the boat and stayed with him. After fishing for an hour or more, my poor gentleman remained fishless, but his friend, in the previously despised pool, had four more salmon.

'We were watching Mr Robson playing the fourth fish when suddenly he staggered backwards and there came a "crack" as the cast broke. Mr Scott was delighted and exclaimed that his friend had been putting far too much strain on the brute anyway, and that it served him right. Then, as we watched, Mr Robson threw down his rod, grabbed the landing-net, dashed into the river, and netted the exhausted fish.

'Mr Scott stood up and shouted: "That's enough. The damn man catches them even when he's lost them!" Picking up his rod, he hurled it into the river and stamped off.

'You'd be surprised how competitive some gentlemen become. I've seen men, friends for years, fall out and argue like children over who should have the right to go down a pool first.

'There's a good lie just up from the cottage, and a fish in it will almost certainly take the first fly offered. Now then, two men, both over seventy, had been fishing here for years. Hearing them in the hotel, you'd have thought them the most considerate creatures on God's earth. But at the river, trying to be first over that lie, they'd act like teenagers pursuing a young lassie, elbowing and shoving, trying to get ahead. And they'd stoop to any device to slow each other down. I've even seen one "accidentally" hide the other's reel or break his cast at the last moment!

'They always used to arrive in the same car, but last time there was such a famous row, that it ended with one

5

of them in the river. One drove home and the other took the train. I was there and saw it all, and I'm as sure as certain that the old gentleman didn't stumble into the river as his friend later claimed. But that was the last we saw of them, or, as I understand it, they of each other.

'But it's not only gentlemen who do strange things. Salmon are just as hard to understand at times. I've watched them in the Till, through Polaroid glasses, following a fly. They'll take it into their mouths, spit it out, take it in again, spit it out, and all without the gentleman being any the wiser.'

I remembered a similar incident myself. For a number of years I used to drive regularly between Newcastle and Edinburgh. Coldstream was about half-way, and the temptation to stop for a look over the Border Bridge was always too great to resist, no matter how important the object of the journey. At times the pool was so packed with salmon that it seemed impossible for another fish to get in. They would lie, ranked like school-children at their desks, awaiting the urge to move upstream.

I have watched an angler putting a fly among them: the fish would move slowly aside to let it pass, and then close ranks. Occasionally, a salmon would follow the fly, as Jim Wallace described, taking it in and then spitting it out, the poor man on the end of the rod knowing nothing of what was happening.

One day, after watching these antics for a while, I flicked a cigarette end over the parapet. The moment the cigarette touched the water a fish of about 15 lb rose to take it. Obviously the salmon hadn't read the Government warning on the side of the packet, but my health certainly suffered all the way to Edinburgh as I tried to fathom it out.

Over the years I have seen many things other than fish caught on flies. A friend, Jim Seaton, while fishing on Loch Leven, ended up with a size fourteen Dunkeld firmly embedded in the point of his nose—and it was a traditional Loch Leven pattern, double-hooked.

He recounts the journey to Edinburgh Royal Infirmary with a wry sense of humour: the puzzled expression on the face of the Forth Road Bridge attendant; his wife, automatically trying to pluck it out on seeing him; the look of disbelief and then suppressed laughter on the part of hospital staff as they told their colleagues to come and look.

But, as Jim Wallace said, 'I've lost count of all the hooks I've removed from ears, noses, backsides, heads, arms and legs. Gentlemen forget that a big salmon fly is a dangerous thing. One ill-considered back-cast reminds them, and spending three hours in hospital rather than in the river makes sure they remember!

'Many of my gillie friends have had nasty accidents with their gentlemen—and they can show you their scars to prove it. I've escaped lightly, because if an angler can't cast properly and safely, I put him ashore to practise until he can. I'll not have such a one in the boat, endangering everything but fish.

'You hear a lot of stories about anglers catching strange things, but I'll tell you one of the strangest, and if you don't believe me, then the gentleman who was with me at the time will be happy to confirm that what I'm saying is true.

'I was fishing the Till here, and after getting my gentleman started, I followed him down the pool. Now the river is only some thirty yards wide, and I was so busy watching how my gentleman was getting on that I made a foolish cast and the flies landed in the long grass on the far bank of the river.

'When I tightened there came a terrible commotion. I'd hooked a partridge under the wing! The bird rose in the air squawking and yelling blue murder. There wasn't much I could do about it, so I pulled it out of the grass, off the bank and into the river.

'Half-way across the river there came this great swirl,

7

and a 12 lb salmon rose and grabbed the dropper. The salmon shot off upstream like a rocket, dragging the partridge after him. At times the salmon and bird were both in the air. When the fish ran, the partridge flapped after him, splashing along the surface; when the salmon sulked, the bird flew helplessly round and round above.

'It took me nearly an hour, but eventually I landed them both. My gentleman was standing watching, mouth agape. He claimed that if he hadn't seen it with his own eyes, he would have called anyone who told him such a story a damned liar. But there you have it, as true as I am sitting here.

'When you've gillied for more than sixty years, you're a hard man to surprise. I've heard most stories, at least once, and well know the ones to believe.'

I told Jimmy about my own strangest catch: telephone wires on Speyside. My father and I were changing beats at Craigellachie, and as we sped along, rods out of the car window, my line got caught on the wires. Within seconds I was down to the backing, and father only just managed to stop before the tip of the rod must surely have been snapped off. Young folk suffer from embarrassment more easily than their seniors, and I still blush at the thought of walking down the middle of the road, in waders, reeling-in to the ribald comments from the occupants of passing cars and coaches.

I asked Jimmy if he had ever lost any of his gentlemen overboard: 'Never, but, mind, there have been one or two I'd have loved to have pushed in. I did once, but it wasn't a gentleman but his lady—a girl really, about twenty-five and a bonny lass. She'd married this older man and they were fishing with me one fine summer day with the sun beating down and not a fish to be seen.

'She was sitting on the fishing stool dressed in a tiny bikini—which is probably why the fish weren't rising—while her husband flogged the water from the bank a hundred yards downstream. I'd been working hard all morning, trying to get the lady a fish, and all she could do was sit there sunning herself and aimlessly waving the rod around.

'Her husband kept calling, telling her to have a splash, so eventually she put down the rod and sat on the stern of the boat, dangling her legs in the water.

'Well, I listened to all this shouting and bawling, rowing hard to keep the boat in position, and just got the toe of my boot behind her and gave a bit of a shove. *Whoosh!* Away she went, right in, like a rocket. Her husband yelled: "What have you done, man? She can't swim!"

quick, because she was in twelve feet of water. Up she came to the surface, spluttering and gasping. I asked her what was wrong and had she swallowed a Jock Scott?

'So I threw her a line, told her to tie it round her waist, and rowed her ashore. But I got a fright when I heard she couldn't swim! Her husband laughed and laughed until he could hardly stand and I thought the lady would take an oar to his head. I heard that they split up not long after that. It was probably as well. She was no hand at the fishing, and far too young for the man, anyway.

'Most of my gentlemen have been easy to work with. If gentlemen listen, then a gillie will do all he can to help them catch fish. But if a gentleman is bad-tempered or rude, then it's a very different matter.

'A gentleman came out with me one morning and I don't think he'd ever fished for salmon before. But to hear him you'd have thought that he'd been at it all his life. When we got to the river, he parked the car and opened the boot.

'Well, I've never seen such a collection of tackle in all my life: at least five rods, box after box of flies, reels, landing-nets, gaffs, body-waders, thigh-waders, coats, hats, jackets, jumpers—and most of it with the price tag still on.

' "Do you think I've forgotten anything?" he asked.

"I called at Pall Mall and they said they'd sort me out properly."

'As it happened, it was one of those rare days when everything was perfect: water temperature, air temperature, water height, not too bright, and fish showing all over the pool. He got the hang of casting right enough, and within minutes had a fish on. After a terrible struggle I netted a good fish of about 12 lb. You could have offered him a million pounds for his place in the boat and it wouldn't have been enough.

'By lunch we had five fish in the boat and he was chatting away like an old hand, mostly about his own skill and wondering why it took some folk years to catch a salmon. The fact that I'd been putting him over the fish and the salmon were almost giving themselves up didn't enter his head. The afternoon was every bit as good, and we ended the day with fifteen beautiful fish.

'As we came ashore, he turned to me and said, in a low, confidential sort of voice, "Wallace, do you see that tree over there on the far bank?"

'I'd been seeing it for damn near forty years, but just answered, "Aye Sir."

' "And that big moss-covered rock?"

' "Aye."

' "Well, that's where the salmon lie. Take a tip from me: if you want your guests to catch fish, put them there!"

'I thanked him kindly and carried the fish ashore. But he was getting a bit cocky by then and told me not to kill the last salmon. He called to his wife to bring the camera, but by the time she'd arrived the fish had flapped itself back into the river. I can see him yet: he took hold of the rod and began bashing it on the ground.

' "What are you doing, Sir?" I asked.

' "I'm battering that damned fly for letting that salmon get away!"

'At night in the hotel he lectured anyone who would listen on the art of salmon fishing. Every salmon was

10

hooked, played and landed ten times over before he went to bed. But by the end of his two weeks he was not half so cocky. He hadn't touched another fish, try as he would.

'On the morning he left he complained to me: "I just can't understand it, Jimmy. I tried everything."

' "Well", I replied, "I'm pleased that you understand that you don't understand. That's a fair way along the road to understanding salmon fishing. But I'm thinking you'll have a much longer journey before you can ever call yourself an angler!"

'But at least the gentleman had learned something, probably the most important lesson of all: there's nothing as certain as the uncertainty of salmon fishing!

'But the rudest man I ever had the misfortune to be with was a grocer from somewhere in Northumberland. He was a big, fat man, gone to seed, and clad in loud breeks that matched his voice. I was walking towards the hotel one morning and there he was standing on the steps waiting: "Hoy!" he bawled. "Are you Wallace?"

'I ignored him and just walked on.

' "Are you Wallace?" he shouted again.

'When I got to the steps, I said: "Aye Sir, that is my name."

' "What's wrong with your hearing then? Didn't you hear me?"

' "I heard you roaring fine. The folk in Berwick probably heard you, too."

' "Well, you're with *me* today, so let's get started. There's no time to waste."

'I walked past him into the hotel and waited out the full half-hour until the time we were officially supposed to start. When I went out I said to him: "Now, look here, Sir. Let's get one matter straight before we go any further: I am not with *you*. You are with *me* and that's the way it will have to be if you want a gillie this day."

' "Have it any way you choose, but get in the car and let's get started."

11

'He had a great big Austin Princess, and on the way down to the river he asked me who the idiot was who lost the six fish the day before and how was he so stupid?

' "Idiot is it?" I replied. "It was the Laird. Nor is he stupid, and he lost them just as easy as that."

' "Well, if tackle counts for anything, I have the lot, and it's the best there is."

'When we arrived at the river, out he jumped and was scrabbling around in the boot of the car like a broody hen. I wasn't surprised when he handed me a spinning rod and a jar of prawns.

' "Here, get this put up", he ordered.

'Now the water was in perfect condition for the fly, but as I might, he wouldn't listen to me and insisted that the spinning rod be put up.

'When I pulled the line from the spool, it snapped. I pulled some more off, and it snapped again. "Look here, Sir. This line is rotten. It's breaking like thread."

' "Nonsense, that's 30 lb breaking-strain."

' "30lb!" I cried. "We pull trees out with that, not salmon!"

'It was all he had, so I made up the cast and off we went. After the first cast the whole thing landed on the water coiled up like a spring, prawn in the middle.

' "Now, Sir. This will never do. We fish for them here, not try to snare the bloody things!"

'Eventually, I managed to straighten the cast, and after a while, a salmon grabbed it. My gentleman just sat there, doing nothing. He turned to me and shouted at me to get on the oars. When I asked why, he replied: "Row man, play the fish!"

' "What fish, Sir?" I asked.

'The salmon had long since gone!

'I told him that was what happened when he didn't pay attention and watch the line all the time.

' "You look after the boat and I'll look after the line."

'He'd have none of it, and said that if I'd been quicker on the oars, then he wouldn't have lost the salmon.

'I mounted another prawn, and in spite of what I'd said, my gentleman sat there, staring up into the sky and paying no attention to the river. When the second fish grabbed for the prawn it was on and off again in a flash, just like the first one.

' "I've told you to watch your line, Sir. Will you not do so?"

' "It's not me that's lost these fish. You've put up the wrong rod, that's the trouble."

' "Rod be damned. It was you that lost the fish, neither the rod nor me."

' "I'll not lose the next one."

' "There might not be a next one", I replied.

'Nor was there. He thrashed away all day, cursing the fish, prawns, flies, weather and me, but never touched another thing. He was as nasty a piece of work as I've ever had the misfortune to be in a boat with. When we got back to the hotel I just walked off, but he called me back. He got out his wallet and opened it, making sure that I saw how full it was.

' "Now, Wallace, here is my business card and personal telephone number. Whenever you think the river is in condition, give me a ring and I'll come right up. Don't forget. I'll make it worth your while."

'I never said a word, but took the card from him, tore it down the middle and chucked it in the gutter at his feet. And that, thank God, was the last we ever saw of him. If I'd ever had him in a boat again, I'd have gladly drowned the blighter!'

Another gentleman Jimmy remembers with little pleasure was a pig-breeder. Jimmy had mounted a small golden sprat and was ordered to take it off and mount a huge silver Devon. This lure was fished all week, but the gentleman caught nothing. On the last day he complained to Jimmy that everyone else in the hotel was catching fish but himself.

'I'm going to the Eden tomorrow. What should I do?'

13

Jimmy replied, 'If I may say so, Sir, the Eden is the best place for you. After the way you've behaved this week, you'll get no help from any gillie here.'

Jimmy never saw the gentleman again.

Another of Jimmy's awkward customers was a manufacturer of billiards-tables. When Jimmy reported for duty he was told that he would have to seek employment elsewhere, since the gentleman intended to fish by himself. So Jimmy worked with a gentleman who had arrived unexpectedly, but kept a careful eye on the lone angler. He was off at the crack of dawn and always last back in the evenings. It was a good week and most of the rods were taking fish each day, but, day after day, the billiards-table king came back blank.

At the end of the week, on the Saturday morning, Jimmy was working in his garden when a Rolls-Royce pulled up outside. Out stepped the fishless angler, and Jimmy, knowing full well that the gentleman had not touched a single salmon, asked politely how he had fared.

'Man, I've not had a single fish, and I'm going home this evening. I was wondering if you might like to come down to the river and have a few casts with me?'

Jimmy replied: 'Well, Sir, you didn't want a gillie at the start of the week, so surely you'll not be wanting the likes of me at the end of it.'

But the gentleman was insistent, and so Jimmy agreed to go down later, when he had finished in the garden.

About four o'clock Jimmy walked down to see how the gentleman was getting on. He found him casting away like a man possessed, but still fishless. When he saw Jimmy, he asked what he should do. Jimmy asked for the rod, mounted an inch-and-a-half silver-and-blue Devon, and within a half-hour had landed two salmon.

The gentleman was most upset and demanded to know what Jimmy had been using.

'Now, Sir, would you give your billiards-tables away for nothing? I doubt it. All I have to offer is my knowledge of this river. It's taken me a lifetime to acquire, so d'you think I should give it away freely? If you'll excuse me, I've work to finish in the garden.'

Jimmy had a look later. At eight o'clock the man was still thrashing away, and still fishless.

The point Jimmy was making was a valid one. Too many anglers expect, and often demand, that a gillie should tell them all he knows. On many waters the gillie is paid only when he works: no fishing guest, no pay. It is wrong, indeed rude, for an angler to expect him to impart specialised information freely to all-comers.

Jimmy Wallace explained: 'You were very poorly paid as a gillie, and never for a six-day week. Some weeks were better than others with tips; but it depended on who the gentlemen were and how many fish they caught. At one time, when I was on the Till, I had three gentlemen every day. Old Colonel White used to arrive with his chauffeur and say, "Don't bother with me, Jimmy. Burroughs will look after me. You take care of the others. It will be the same at the end of the week."

'Now it's a different sort of breed of gentleman—all commercial. All they seem to want is more and more fish to sell to pay for their holiday.'

I asked Jimmy who were the finest casters he had worked with. He remembered particularly Mr MacNaught, from Dunblane, who had a large department store in Glasgow. Mr MacNaught was a man of sixteen stones and he used a sixteen foot rod to match his weight. Jimmy would hear him muttering as he cast: 'Get out you bugger!'

Then there was a young geologist from Aberdeen, Mr Milne, who always fished with tiny treble hooks and was one of the best casters Jimmy has ever worked with.

But one of Jimmy's favourite gentlemen was old Mr Crawford, who called himself 'the banana king'.

'They call me the "banana king", Jimmy, because I brought the first bananas into Britain.'

Mr Crawford fished with Jimmy for years, and at the grand old age of 84 was still a regular visitor. Mr Crawford and Jimmy would sit at the fishing hut, yarning, smoking and dramming, and never cast a line. At lunchtime, when Mrs Crawford arrived, she would ask how the morning had gone. 'Not a bloody bite, Maggie, not a bite.'

After lunch Mrs Crawford would leave and he would turn and say to Jimmy: 'Right, down to the bottom of the beat, Jimmy, and gie me your coat and cushion. I'll have a bit of a sleep while you have a cast.'

At four o'clock Jimmy would wake the old gentleman and they would row back up river to be met once more by Mrs Crawford.

'How's it gone then, Jack?' she would enquire.

'Not a damned fish down there, Maggie, not a fish.'

For the first twenty years that Jimmy Wallace fished there were no such things as Waddingtons. The orthodox patterns such as Jock Scott, Thunder and Lightning and Dusty Miller were used. On dull days a Black Doctor used to do well, as did that old Tweed stand-by, Silver Wilkinson.

'I don't think we killed as many fish with the old single-hooked patterns as we do now with tube-flies', said Jimmy, 'but it was far more fun—no lead weight, just bang it out—and that took some doing with the heavy Tweed rods. Now they just strip off line and throw it like a bait. That's not fly-fishing. I've tried to tell them: that's not fly-fishing.'

One of the most useful Tweed patterns in recent years has been the Munro Killer, but when Jimmy first saw the fly he had little confidence in it. But he was fishing one autumn in high water and his gentleman insisted on using a small Munro Killer. They landed three fish before lunch. Jimmy was converted.

Jimmy has always maintained that ladies are far more demanding than gentlemen, and, generally, much better, or much luckier, anglers. He explained that a lady will have you working away from dawn to dusk, whereas a gentleman will stop for a smoke and a blether. But the ladies are most persistent. One of the best and most successful of Jimmy's lady anglers is the Laird's wife, Lady Burnett, who took one of the heaviest fish caught in recent years, a 43 lb salmon from the Pot Pool.

'What time is it Jimmy?' Lady Burnett will enquire.

'Two minutes to go, Madam.'

'Good! Time for another few casts!'

And more often than not, Jimmy says, there will be another fish on the bank before finishing time.

Jimmy once gillied for a retired colonel and his wife, and remembers the colonel's lady as being no lightweight: 'Fifteen stone if an ounce, and the whole of her behind covered the fishing stool. The lady was so strong she used a big Tweed rod and punched the line, straight out, into the teeth of the wildest storm.'

The lady never seemed to notice the weather. Wind, rain, hail, snow, sleet or flood, she concentrated on the job in hand with single-minded determination. And the moment a salmon touched her fly, she would leap up and give the rod an almighty yank.

'Dear God, Lady!' Jimmy would exclaim. 'If you hit the poor creatures as hard as that, you'll have one come flying from the river and knock you overboard.'

'Rubbish, Jimmy! You have to let them know from the start who's in charge.'

The best Jimmy could do was to keep his wits about him and his head well down. But by the end of the day the colonel's lady had hooked six fish and landed every one. Her husband had slaved away all day without a touch.

In the bar before dinner the colonel asked Jimmy how his wife had got on, and if she had lost any fish.

'Lose them!' Jimmy exploded. 'She hooked them so hard that she damned near pulled their heads clean off. You'll have to tell her, Sir, to be more gentle with them.'

But the colonel was not keen on the idea and suggested

17

that such advice would be far better coming from Jimmy than from himself.

'Look, I have to make a telephone call. Here she comes. You have a word with her while I'm gone.'

But Jimmy held his peace.

'I was not that brave, nor that stupid—which is why I'm still alive and able to tell the tale now!'

It was with a sense of real regret that I made my farewells to Twizel Bridge and Jimmy Wallace—as fine a gentleman as any of the gentlemen he ever worked for, and one of the most knowledgeable and likeable personalities it has been my privilege to meet.

CHAPTER 2

Hebridean charm and the Heather Isles

Ann and I sailed from Uig, on the Island of Skye, across the broken waters of the Minch. Behind us was a distant prospect of the snow-capped Cuillins; westwards, the Outer Hebrides, the 'Long Island'—Lewis, 'the heather isle'; mountainous Harris; loch-scattered North Uist and Benbecula, 'the hill of the fords'; and gentle South Uist, with its shining white sands and wild-flower-clad machair lands.

Even today the islands retain most of their ancient traditions and identity. Evidence of change there is, but it is a slow, orderly adaptation of custom, rather than a frenetic charge to the future.

Our destination was Lochmaddy on North Uist; our purpose, to meet Charles MacLean, one of the last of the Hebridean gillies on the South Uist Estate at Lochboisdale.

19

An added attraction was that we were to stay on Benbecula with our son, Blair, and his wife, Barbara.

We first visited the Uists and Benbecula in 1977, and fell in love with their beauty, serenity and calm. Six years later, Blair chose to live and work there: 'When I go to work in the morning, I see the hills of Harris to the north; westwards, out in the Atlantic, St Kilda; to the south, Hecla and Beinn Mhor; and eastwards, the Cuillins. I think I'm very lucky.'

The Uists and Benbecula offer some of the finest game-fishing in the world. They have hundreds of freshwater lochs. Many, such as Scadavy, Fada and Obisary, are such a wild scatter that one loch can seem to be an endless number of different waters. The shoreline of Scadavy meanders in and out, round headlands and bays, for a distance of more than fifty miles. It has more than 200 little islands, and some of these even have their own lochans. Fada and Obisary present the same wonderful prospect of islands, promontories and fishy corners.

You really have to see it to believe it, but nearly half of North Uist is covered by lochs, and one of the most exciting is Loch nan Geireann, in the north of the island, full of hard-fighting brown trout, silvery sea-trout and salmon covered with sea-lice. Neolithic pottery remains were found in such quantity on one of the small islands in the loch that it is probable that the kilns there supplied the whole community.

We drove southwards from Lochmaddy to Benbecula across the North Ford, where the sea surges, emerald-green and crystal-clear against the stones of the causeway, opened by the Queen Mother in 1960. The flat moorland landscape is dominated by Ruival, the only hill on the island. Here, in June 1746, in a shallow cave, Bonnie Prince Charlie anxiously waited for Flora MacDonald. Flora's step-father, Captain Hugh MacDonald, was guarding the South Ford, and it was he who arranged the necessary travel documents which allowed the Prince to escape disguised as Flora's maid, Betty Burke. Had Bonnie Prince Charlie been content with taking a few fish, rather than a king's throne, a lot of heads would have remained on a lot of shoulders, and he would have had a far less taxing journey through the mountains and moorlands of the Hebrides.

The islanders are renowned for their wry sense of humour and careful attention to opportunity. In many ways they resemble my own community in Caithness. It's easy enough to be fancy-free in the more hospitable climate of the south, where services and facilities are ready to hand, but in the remote corners of our land many of these things are luxuries. People tend to be careful.

I was talking to one of the engineering officers with the Army at Balivanich, on Benbecula. A few years back he organised an exercise to recover the many abandoned vehicles that litter roadside and fields. Over a weekend, he and his soldiers collected more than fifty 'heaps' and cleared them away. First thing the following Monday morning, a queue of disgruntled islanders formed outside his office, demanding to know who had stolen their vehicles and what compensation was to be expected. The Major learned his lesson and left well alone in future.

When George and Irene Pert moved into the Lochmaddy Hotel on North Uist, one of their first callers was a well-known local worthy—well-known, that is, to everyone else, but not to the new arrivals.

'Good morning, Mr Pert, and what a fine day it is. Welcome to Lochmaddy. I'm your dustbin-man.'

George asked what service he performed and was told that, once a week, he came and moved the dustbins down to the side of the road. After emptying, he took them in again, a distance of perhaps ten yards.

'And how much does that cost me?' George enquired.

'Surely, nearly nothing at all—only ten pounds a week.'

Being a cautious man, George 'enquired', only to find that the man had never moved anything heavier than a well-filled pint tumbler, and that only as far as his mouth!

The 'water of life' plays a large part in the lives of many islanders. Indeed, if my memory serves me correctly, the Greagory Hotel once held the world record for the amount of whisky consumed in the space of one evening. When my wife and I dropped in for a quick one, in 1977, we were amazed to see, behind the bar, a long row of neat brown paper bags—pre-packed carry-outs to save time at the end of the evening!

But the most famous event concerning whisky took place on a stormy morning in February 1941 when the *SS Politician* ran aground off Roshinish Point, between Calvay Island and Eriskay. Number 5 hold contained 25,000 cases of whisky: Spey Royal, Ballantine's, Haig's, MacCullum's, and many more. Duncan MacInnes was a boy of fifteen at the time and spending the week working aboard his father's boat, *St Winifred*. After several visits to the *Polly*, as she affectionately became known, they were stormbound in Lochboisdale.

'I remember MacColl, the Customs man in Lochboisdale, coming on board and enquiring why the lads didn't go to the hotel for a drink. I'm sure they had some excuse about the fishing being poor, but he left in high spirits with a generous fry of flounders and whistling *Annie Laurie*.'

Compton MacKenzie's glorious book, *Whisky Galore*, well documents that happy wreck, and pride of place is still given in the bar of the Lochboisdale Hotel to a huge photograph of the luckless *SS Politician*.

Rose-Ann Smiley, from the hotel, had arranged my meeting with Charles MacLean, so I called to thank her. I paid homage to the *SS Politician* at one of the longest bars I have ever seen—some forty feet of it! Such a bar was necessary in the days of the whaling industry. Vessels sought refuge in the bay after long months at sea, and their thirsty crews would descend on Lochboisdale, clamouring for instant attention. A fair bit of clamouring was going on when I was there, never mind days of yore, so I beat a hasty retreat to Charlie MacLean's cottage, a few miles up the road towards Daliburgh.

Charlie MacLean was born on the island of Tiree. He is a gentle, soft-spoken man with an accent redolent of heather and hills. During a busy life he has seen and done much, including six years in the South Atlantic with the whaling fleets. Neither he nor his wife keep good health these days, but they greeted me with typical island courtesy and cheerfulness. We sat before a blazing peat fire, an April gale howling outside, and I asked Charlie about his days as a gillie.

'You have to concentrate for a very long time indeed to understand your lochs and gentlemen. Even after thirty years, I still find I'm learning every time I go out. That's what makes the whole thing so enjoyable: you can never predict what will happen. Let me give an example ...

'Some years ago a party of sportsmen was staying at Greagory Lodge. Twelve of the guests fished, so every evening names were drawn from a hat to decide who should have which loch the following day, and I had to gillie for the folk who drew West Loch Ollay.

'Now this is a very good loch, a machair loch, near Ormiclate Castle, about three-quarters of a mile long by half-a-mile wide, and with trout that average more than 2 lb. Well, we fished that loch all week, each day with a different gentleman, and no matter how hard we tried, we never touched a fish. You can imagine that, come Friday evening, no one was anxious to fish 'that' loch again.

'The gentleman who drew West Loch Ollay arrived at the lochside on the Saturday morning looking very despondent. But by the end of the day it was an entirely different matter: eighteen beautiful fish were in the boat, not one less than 2 lb. We took trout from all over the loch: by the islands, in the shallows, along the weed-beds, in the deep—as perfect a basket of trout I have never seen, before or since. Nor have I ever seen such a happy smile on a man's face. My gentleman could hardly wait to show off his catch at the Lodge.

'What a commotion there was then, and it was mostly coming in my direction: I hadn't taken them to the right places; I'd put up the wrong flies; it was all my fault that they hadn't got good baskets as well. So I asked my gentleman to show his friends exactly where we'd been fishing. They trooped through to the big map on the wall, and my gentleman pointed out exactly where we'd taken the fish—and weren't they the very same places where we'd been fishing all week!

'But the fish were on their tails that day and no mistake. We were just lucky to be in the right place at the right time, for no matter how well you know a loch, if the fish aren't in the mood, there's nothing you can do about it other than to keep on trying and trusting to luck.'

I remembered my own recent experience of fishing Mid and East Loch Ollay. After five hours I had decided to re-name the lochs 'Sugar Ollay' and 'Dam Ollay', only to find that my wife, Ann, had caught half-a-dozen lovely fish. There is little justice in the world.

Charlie paused and we mused silently upon the vagaries of trout. I poured two generous measures of eighteen-year-old Old Pultney and passed one over to Charlie.

'But if you get a suitable day, then you'll catch fish. Well, here's your good health. You know, there's a gentleman comes fishing with me and he always brings a very fine whisky with him, just like this. You feel it going down, warming you, right to your toes.'

I agreed.

The machair lochs of South Uist produce high-quality brown trout. They have an abundance of food—freshwater shrimps and snails—and they are shallow lochs, warming up quickly in the early months of the season, encouraging great activity among trout and anglers alike.

Everywhere in Scotland, people complain that fishing is not as good as it was. But this is not so as far as the machair lochs are concerned. In fact, many of them are over-stocked. An Edinburgh doctor was recently asked to keep all the fish he caught during the course of a day. He took more than seventy trout. Each year, expert local anglers are invited to fish, and even with their efforts, it's difficult to maintain the proper balance between numbers of fish and feeding, in order to keep the average weight high. Excellent baskets of trout are taken: twelve fish weighing 25 lb from West Loch Ollay; twenty-one trout weighing 17½ lb from Loch Altabrugh; and many more from waters such as Kildonan, Bornish, Stilligarry and Grogarry. The fishing is every bit as good as it was in 'the old days', and the trout are just as beautiful, too.

Over the years Charlie's gentlemen have returned again and again to fish with him. Many are great friends and fishing companions as well as guests. But it's not always plain sailing. There are always one or two who are difficult and refuse to listen to advice.

'To be honest, you have to be out in a boat with a gentleman only for half-an-hour to tell whether or not he's a sportsman', said Charlie. 'And if he's not, then a gillie soon lets him know!

'An accountant from Glasgow was up here once and wanted a day on Loch Bornish. We'd hardly been fishing for a minute when he spotted a trout rising at the other side of the loch and told me to row away over. No sooner were we there than he saw a fish rising near the island. Away we went again. Then one rose exactly where we had started. Back we went! For nearly two hours, I was rowing round the loch like a galley slave, so eventually, I just rowed ashore.

' "What d'you think you're doing?" he said. "Where d'you think you're going, MacLean?"

' "Going? Going?" says I, "I'm getting out of this boat and going home. I'm not a bliddy steam-engine, to be rowing you from one side of the loch to the other all day. I told you when we started that you'll catch fish all over this loch. No one place is better than another. Now, if you'll not take heed, then there's no point in my being here, so you may do what you please."

'That quietened him down a bit and he behaved himself for the rest of the day. But I had a word with the factor in the evening, so the gentleman got the sharp edge of the factor's tongue as well!'

One of Charlie's friends has his own method of dealing with difficult gentlemen. He was out once with a guest and soon discovered that the gentleman had taken no whisky with him.

'What did you do?' enquired Charlie.

'Well, I just took him to where there were no fish!'

It is almost a tradition of fishing that you take along some 'comfort' for the hard-working gillie. Not to do so is considered rude. Even worse is to have a dram yourself without offering one to the gillie. A gentleman was fishing on Loch Tay and after he had caught his first salmon he took out his hip-flask and helped himself to a mighty swig, but didn't offer one to his gillie. The same happened after he had taken a second fish, and a third. It was a cold, wet day, and when the gentleman decided to have a cigar, he couldn't find anything dry on which to strike a match.

'MacDonald, have you anything dry where I can strike this match?' he asked.

Stroking his throat, MacDonald replied instantly: 'Try here, Sir, try here!'

But, as Charlie explained, difficult gentlemen are few and far between. Most of the guests are only too ready to listen to advice: to pass the rod to the gillie to give him a few casts, or to help on the oars if there is a sudden squall. He once had a famous pop-star and his wife out on School House Loch. They were both keen to catch a sea-trout, and they started early in the morning, with a cold north-east wind for company, and fished on, hour after hour, but without seeing so much as a fin.

In the afternoon the wind blew even harder and it began

to rain, so by a quarter to five, everyone had had enough. Cold, frozen and fishless, the gentleman turned to Charlie and asked where the nearest hotel was.

'Greagory', Charlie replied.

'Well, for God's sake, let's go there!'

The boat was turned and they headed for shore with the gentleman still casting away in a half-hearted fashion. Ten yards from the jetty there was a tremendous splash. He had hooked a huge sea-trout which almost pulled him out of the boat with its first mad rush. It went off like a rocket and had him near down to the backing twice before Charlie managed to net it: 7 lb, and still with sea-lice.

For devilment, Charlie took up the oars and continued to make for the shore.

'What's wrong? Why are we going in?'

'It's the nearest hotel you were wanting, was it not?'

'No, no! Stop! Let's try another drift!'

By seven o'clock six more fish were in the boat. The smallest weighed 5 lb and the heaviest, 9 lb. The gentleman and his lady had had a day to remember, and that evening no happier folk were on all the Hebrides.

The heaviest sea-trout caught on South Uist was a superb fish of 14 lb, and a cast of it is displayed in the Lochboisdale Hotel. It was caught by a ten-year-old boy, a relation of the Laird. During the same week he also had his first stag—another day to remember!

One day Charlie will never forget. He was fishing Kildonan with Dr Robertson when the doctor hooked a large sea-trout. He played it for more than an hour. At last, the fish tired. The doctor drew it across the surface towards the boat and asked Charlie for the landing-net. Charlie tucked the oars under his knees and handed over the net.

The fish was coming in perfectly, exhausted and played out—or so it seemed. But when it saw the boat, it gave one last, mighty leap over an oar and broke the cast. At times like that, there is nothing to be said: it's final. Charles and Dr Robertson shared a commiseratory dram and went home. They estimated the fish weighed more than 15 lb and would certainly have been a new record for the islands. Such is fishing, and nothing is more true than the fact that it is always the biggest fish that gets away!

Charles MacLean has a great love for and knowledge of the islands' wild-life. Each of the South Uist lochs is like a miniature nature reserve. There seems always to be a pair of mute swans disdainfully watching your efforts; or visiting whooper swans, from far-off Iceland; or a heron, statue-like at the water's edge; or greylag, white-fronted and barnacle geese; or flights of duck whisking by; or redshank, curlew, golden plover and gulls calling. And, as darkness falls, the harsh, 'rusty-engined' grating of the corncrake follows you home.

The Hebrides are one of the last remaining bastions of the otter, and a short distance from Charlie's cottage is a track which otters use when coming up from the sea. They are delightful animals, and many years ago the local postman in Lochboisdale had one as a pet. The beast used to follow him everywhere, even into the pub.

A less-welcome visit from an otter occurred more recently. One of Charlie's gentlemen had been having a difficult day at the sea-trout, managing, after hours of hard work, to catch only one good fish of about 4 lb. Exhausted by his effort, he put the fish down beside him and had a snooze. When he woke up, the sea-trout had gone. Leading to the river were the tell-tale pug-marks of a large otter. That was another one-that-got-away story!

Local produce figures largely in the South Uist diet: salmon, sea-trout, trout, lobsters, clams and cormorants. I was surprised when I heard of that last delicacy. Mrs MacLean had served tea and was talking about eating habits when she mentioned it. I knew that the former inhabitants of St Kilda used to eat gulls, as they still do in the Faroe Islands—but cormorants?

'Would you like the recipe?' asked Mrs MacLean.
'Why ... er ... yes, please', I said politely.

'Well, you want a young cormorant; and skin it—don't try to pluck it. Clean it and then stuff an onion in it to remove the oily flavour. Bury the bird under three feet of sand for two weeks. Dig it up, throw away the bird and eat the onion!'

Yes, I fell for it, too! But Mrs MacLean told the story with such a straight face that I believed it until the very last moment!

Charlie was busy as a gillie until 1983, when ill-health confined him to the fireside. His wife never fished, but over the years Charlie had to contend with many ladies out on the loch.

'But you've got to have the patience for it,' he said, 'and my eyes are getting bad for tying up new casts all day and sorting out fankles. I had two ladies out with me one day, and neither of them had fished before. So I took them to Upper Kildonan, where there's always a good chance of fish. I gave them a single fly each, on a short cast, and told them what to do.

'After a while, they got tired of thrashing about and were just trailing the flies through the water. D'you know, they caught five or six fish each like that, and every day afterwards it was them hurrying down to the loch, not me! They were as keen as keen could be. One morning, when there was too much teasing and not enough fishing, one of them went over the side. What a job we had getting her back in the boat! But she fished on, all day. Soaked though she was!'

Some of the South Uist lochs can be windy and dangerous, so Charlie makes sure that his gentlemen behave themselves—and the ladies, too! He was out on Loch Fada with Mrs Smiley and Mrs Russel when a particularly strong wind got up. The ladies were both expert fishers, but, as luck would have it, each hooked a fish at the same time. Charlie couldn't do much to help, since it was taking all his strength just to keep the nose of the boat into the wind.

Pandemonium reigned. The fish ran and jumped, first one way, then the other, then both the same way. Rods were handed round as if it were passing-the-parcel at a children's party, and it was a miracle they didn't become entangled. Charlie somehow managed to land both fish: a perfectly-matched brace of sea-trout weighing 7 lb apiece.

Like most gillies, the time Charlie dreaded most was when a loch went dour. Guests had often come hundreds of miles to fish, so he felt it was his duty to make sure they didn't go home empty-handed. On one such occasion, to save the day, Charlie improvised.

After finishing his lunchtime beer, he stuck a length of strong nylon into the bottle and jammed it in place with the cork. To the other end of the nylon, he attached a size ten Black Pennell. With a mighty heave, he threw the whole lot out into the loch.

No sooner had the fly touched the surface than it was grabbed and the bottle set off at a great rate, being towed behind a startled sea-trout. Charlie and another gillie set off in hot pursuit in the boat, one rowing like mad, the other in the bows with landing-net poised. After a mad chase round the loch, accompanied by much shouting and cheering from the bank, they safely netted a fish of nearly 5 lb. It was the only fish of the day.

Some of Charlie's gentlemen had their own methods of attracting fish when things were quiet. The strangest method Charlie saw was practised by Ian Christie, a solicitor from Portree, on the Island of Skye. Two gentlemen were in the boat with Charlie at the time: Ian Christie himself, and Kenny McKinnon.

It had been a long day, with not much doing, and hope of a good basket was fading fast. Ian Christie had a small cassette player with him and a tape of Gaelic melodies, sung by Callum Kennedy. So, to pass the time, he turned on the recorder. There was still no sign of fish. But then the beautiful song, *My brown-haired girl*, was sung, and up came as beautiful a trout to grab Ian Christie's fly.

No further fish rose, so when the tape was finished, they played it again. The moment the strains of *My brown-haired girl* floated over the loch, up came another trout to take the fly.

That was too much of a coincidence, so they rewound the tape until just before the magic melody. Sure enough, up came a fish looking for action. During the course of the afternoon they tried several other tunes on the fish, but they liked nothing other than *My brown-haired girl*. It was played again and again and again, and each time it produced a fish until they called it a day.

It's a story which is hard to swallow—unless, of course, it's happened to you.

Many years ago, I was fishing at Manor Water on Tweed. After three hours I was still fishless and starting to think that I would be going back to Edinburgh with an empty basket. Music has always played an important part in my life, and at that time I had just discovered Handel's *Messiah*. I was musing on the possibility of how I would be able to perform the miracle of the loaves and fishes when I was unable to catch one fish, let alone five. I started to sing the aria 'He shall feed his flock' and immediately caught a trout. The longer and louder I sang, the more fish I caught. When I stopped, so did the fish. When I had taken five, I decided that it would be polite to stop. But ever since, when times have been hard on river or loch, guess what tune I've hummed?

It takes an angler to appreciate, understand and believe these stories, for far-fetched though they may sound, they are all true. Charlie and I finished our drams and, for old time's sake, had another.

We drove back to Balivanich in the glorious calm of an Hebridean evening, past mist-shrouded Hecla and over O'Regan's Bridge to Benbecula. There is a special magic about the islands that defies description; and there is a special charm about the people, so beautifully typified by Charles MacLean.

CHAPTER 3

Of 'Wild' Jock McAskill and stags and salmon in the Great Glen

Travel down the south shore of Loch Ness, in the Great Glen, past Castle Urquhart, Invermoriston and Fort Augustus, and you are on an historic road. The area was opened up by General Wade from 1725. During seven years, with a team of 500 men, he completed 240 miles of road and thirty bridges throughout the Highlands.

Press on, following the ribbon of Telford's Caledonian Canal to Loch Oich, stop on the bridge at Invergarry and look downstream. Tucked away in the woods at the side of the tumbling river is a small cottage. It is the home of one of the north's most colourful characters, 'Wild' Jock MacAskill, stalker and gillie, Gaelic scholar and musician, and expert on everything that swims in the river, flies in the air, or lives on the hill.

When I arrived in the late afternoon of a sharp spring day, Jock was busily directing operations to remove a timber roof that had come down in recent gales. Unfortunately, it had fallen on Jock's car, and he was none too pleased.

Task completed, we retired to the fireside and I told Jock my plans for a book about Scottish gillies.

'A greater bunch of rascals you'll not find in all the land—outside of Westminster, that is. And if I don't know what I'm talking about, nobody does. I've been a gillie all my years!'

A recent photograph in the local paper had shown Jock, bright-eyed and smiling, proudly displaying four Loch Oich salmon, each weighing more than 17 lb. Their capture would have been not a bad effort for a youngster, but for a man still working, long after lesser mortals have comfortably retired, it was a remarkable achievement indeed.

With disarming modesty, Jock said he had been lucky: in the right place at the right time. But, as every salmon-fisher knows, there's more to it than luck. Jock's knowledge of the loch, built up over years of experience, is second to none, and few can match his skill.

Jock MacAskill is a man of medium height, stockily built, with the air of one long accustomed to an outdoor life. Indeed, most of his time has been spent on loch, river or hill, and when I asked him if he would change anything, had he the chance to live his life again, he was quick to reply:

'Well, I wouldn't lose that huge salmon in the Chest Pool, or miss that thirteen-pointer on Ben Tee, but, oh yes, I'd do it all again! There's nothing else I'd rather do!'

Jock started keepering as a young man in Perthshire, on the Brae Roy Estate, where his father worked for Mr Scott. Jock's father asked if he could have a lad for the hill, and that's how Jock began to learn about stalking.

'Few things are more enjoyable or more exciting, and the longer the stalk, the better I like it', he said.

The Brae Roy head-keeper was getting on in years, although he could still out-walk a man half his age. Jock remembers his tall, rangey figure striding up the hill. When the old man's eyesight began to fail, he would turn to Jock and say: 'Now then lad, give me a good nudge if you see anything.'

Jock learned the ways of the hill from watching and listening as the stalkers took their gentlemen in. He began to realise how observant a stalker had to be; not only for deer, but to discover his gentlemen's capabilities. Older gentlemen had to be paced carefully. There was little point in arriving at the stag, if your gentleman was miles behind, out of breath, still struggling up the hill. If he wasn't properly rested, then he was hardly likely to hit the mark when the time came.

One morning, Jock was out with General Sir John Ramsden. He was a fine shot, but he always stood up to fire, rather than spying on a stag and shooting it in cold blood, so to speak. That was always his way.

Because the ground was flattish, Jock couldn't get a proper sight of the stags, but away to the right, he spotted a knowe and suggested they made for it. From that vantage point they would be looking down on the deer. It was a long crawl, but eventually they made the high ground. Sure enough, there were the deer, below them. One was an old 'swish'. He'd be first. Another, with a good head, the old hair still on him, wouldn't last the winter. He'd be next.

'Now, Sir, are you ready?'

Up stood the General, and in two shots he had two dead

deer. That was the way with him, and he rarely missed.

The task of outwitting a herd of wild red deer is no easy matter. The beasts are in their natural environment and know, instinctively, every inch of their domain. Getting close enough for a shot, without disturbing them, takes great skill and a complete knowledge of the forest.

Jock explained that what seemed difficult, even impossible, was often second nature to an experienced stalker.

'I know every inch of the forest. I've spent my life there, so it's easy for me to spot the deer and know how to get to them. But gentlemen new to the hill have to take their time, and one of the quickest ways of finding out how much they know is to watch them using the spy-glass. If they get into a good position easily, then they'll probably do just as well when the time comes for a shot. If not, then you have to offer advice and assistance.

'When I spot a herd, I always tell my gentleman which beast we're going for and make him study it through the glass. Far better that than have him shoot the wrong stag. During a difficult stalk all he may see, for several hours, are the soles of my boots as he crawls along behind. I tell him where we're going to shoot from, how we'll get there, how the wind will affect our progress, and point out danger spots along the way.

'The length of time a stalk takes depends on many things. If a stag has hinds with him, then it'll be much more difficult. There'll always be an old hind, watching, watching, keeping an eye on you, protecting the stag. The stalker has to know how to get past her to the stag, and if his gentleman isn't very experienced, then it's even harder.

'You may have told him all you can: to crawl when you crawl; to stop when you stop. He may indeed be trailing along behind, nose to the ground, doing his best; but if his backside's up in the air, the hind will spot it immediately.

'Or she might see the heel of your gentleman's boot as

he comes snaking along; or his shoulder as he tumbles into a hollow. She'll be suspicious, and watch and watch, stare and stare. You'll lie there, cramped and aching, hoping your gentleman is doing the same, until she settles.

'You have to be patient. When she turns away, the moment you move, she's back, watching, trying to catch you. Now if she has a calf, you may get past by showing yourself to him. He'll be frightened and run to mammy. She'll know he's scared, search round with her great eyes, and then, maybe, move far enough to let you through.

'A stalker has to understand these things and choose his ground accordingly; understand the wind; know the corries where the deer are; how the wind blows into them. There's nothing more exasperating, after a long, difficult stalk, than to see your stag crossing the march boundary on to your neighbour's forest because of some ill-considered action that's put him on his guard. Then you've lost him. I'd never go on to another man's ground. That's a thing I've never done and would never condescend to do.

'If a stalker really knows what he's doing, that shouldn't happen; and if the deer are over the march, then it's sometimes possible to bring them back anyway, without leaving your own forest. One morning I had two gentlemen out with me and I quickly realised that they hadn't much idea what it was all about.

'Nor were they the type to listen. They jabbered away up the hill until they'd exhausted themselves and me with their blethers. Fine company I'll have today, I thought to myself.

'Anyway, away we went, up the hill to the first spying point. Nothing. The deer were all over the march. So I decided what to do and soon had my gentlemen crawling along behind me. After a while I heard them muttering and cursing. "Good grief! Does the fellow know what he's doing? The wind's behind us! Has he gone soft in the head?"

'I said nothing, but crawled on. You see, I knew most of

the stags were over the boundary in the Sanctuary and wouldn't be coming out until ready to go on the hinds. But it was nearly that time and I was making for Creag Dubh, the Black Rock, where the wind would take our scent to the deer. When we came there I stopped and said: "Now, gentlemen, we'll have a bit of a spy." Resting against a boulder, I took out my pipe and lit up. They struggled with their glasses, not looking at all pleased.

' "You'll be wondering what it is I'm doing this morning?"

'No answer.

' "Well, in a few minutes you'll see what it is I've been trying to achieve." I sat back and enjoyed my smoke.

'Sure enough, after a while, we saw the first horns coming over the boundary on to our ground. Then they all came, and what a grand sight—more than twenty stags, moving quietly over the heather. We had a long stalk because there were so many beasts, but we shot one of the best stags of the season, as grand a royal as any man could wish for, and by evening my gentlemen were beginning to look a lot more like sportsmen than they had in the morning.'

Back at the Lodge, Jock spoke to his two gentlemen.

'Now, Sirs, you'll understand why I was working with a following wind: to bring the deer over the boundary. Tomorrow, gentlemen, save your breath for the stalking and leave the cursing to me.'

And very pleased they were to do so.

During the Second World War Jock was in the Lovat Scouts and his commanding officer was the Laird, Locheil. One year, at the time of the Lochaber Ball, Jock was helping with parking cars when Locheil came over and asked how the stalking was. When Jock explained that the stags were all away over the boundary, Locheil offered to send the shepherds out to bring them back. But Jock has never needed such help. He brings the beasts back by making sure they have his scent. The deer do the rest.

'Using shepherds to move deer is common practice', Jock told me. 'You'll see a shepherd out on the hill, working his dogs and know damn fine that it's not the sheep he's after, but the deer. They put a stag away on me one day, so when the shepherd came over I gave him a piece of my mind. He tried to tell me that he was only working the sheep. "Well", I said, "you'd better go and have your eyes tested. There's not a sheep among that flock that belongs to you. They're all Locheil's."

'But what can you do? Most of them are neighbours and many of them stalkers, too, and you've got to live and work with them. But I was mad, after such a long stalk, to lose the beast like that.'

Three generations of MacAskills have worked at Invergarry, starting with Jock's grandfather in the days of Lord Ward, soldier, statesman and chief of the Metropolitan special constabulary during the First World War.

In the spring of 1895, the Duke of Portland became tenant of the Garry fishings, and Jock's father was gillie when the Duke caught the largest salmon ever taken from Loch Oich—a 44-pounder caught on 23 March, 1907. This great salmon was 4 ft 2 ins long and had a girth of 2 ft 2 ins. That day, the Duke and Jock's father had five fish weighing a total of 115 lb, an average of 23 lb.

But the Garry and Loch Oich have always been famous for the size of their salmon. During one week, in March 1913, the Duke and his guests caught 83 salmon with an average weight of more than 16 lb. '... on the 22nd March, Barker Carr and I and Mr and Mrs Davis killed no less than nineteen. This was a record day for Loch Oich. There was not much snow-water coming down, though the snow was deep on the hills. The wind suddenly veered to the south-west, and the river and loch began to rise very fast in the afternoon. The result was that 19 fish weighing 276 lb, with an average weight of 14 lb, were killed.'

But it was hard work with little reward for the gillies. Jock remembers those difficult days all too well. They were not made any easier by the attitude of some of the gentlemen, who were very demanding most of the time and downright unpleasant for the rest.

In these days, gentlemen expected two gillies: one to carry rod and tackle, the other to carry the fish caught. Short piers stood out into the pools, and the gillie with the rod had to be standing ready, line out, fly in the water, waiting to hand it to the gentleman when he arrived. Unfortunately, it was considered ill-mannered of a gillie to walk ahead of the gentleman, so there was always a last-minute scramble to be in the right place at the right time. Nor was it any easier for the second gillie. He would be struggling along the bank, lumping a sack which might contain anything up to 100 lb of salmon.

Jock remembers his father telling him of a day he spent working with General Paget. The General was a tall, stern man with a prominent nose over a well-groomed moustache. He had served in the Ashanti War, the Sudan, Burma and South Africa, and was Commander-in-chief in Ireland during the troubled times of the Home Rule Bill. He had long legs and a short temper, and none of the gillies liked working with him.

The General would dash from pool to pool, striding ahead, shouting and bawling if the gillie wasn't ready with the rod when he arrived. One morning, on the day the General was due to leave, he decided to have a last couple of hours on the river before the pony and trap took him off to the station. Jock's father was with him and remembers it as being one of those days when the river was full of fish, jumping and splashing in every pool, but quite uninterested in taking a fly, no matter what was offered.

Jock's father was changing flies after almost every cast, and the General was becoming more and more bad-tempered. He had a large selection of flies, all beautifully dressed, in a mahogany box. Eventually, he turned to Mr MacAskill and snapped: 'Pack up. I have to go. But leave the fly-box out.'

When everything was neatly away, the General took the fly-box, walked to the end of a pier, opened the box and threw its contents into the river.

'There you are, you damned brutes!' he shouted. 'Take your bloody choice!'

With that he turned his back on Jock's father and stamped off without so much as a thank-you or goodbye. But it was an ill wind ... For days afterwards, the gillies were picking up salmon flies from the river, and at nearly £1 a time, they were some consolation for all the trouble the General had given them.

The biggest salmon Jock has had to his own rod was a 40 lb fish from Loch Oich. This was in the days before the Garry hydro-electric scheme, and like most of the gillies I spoke to, Jock had few kind words to say about the Hydro Board.

'No matter what people say, they've ruined the fishing here. The fish-ladder at Loch Garry is just experimental. Salmon are stripped, eggs hatched and fry eventually taken by helicopter out to the burns. But the gulls and mergansers eat them. In all the years I've fished here, I've never once seen a tagged fish return to the river.'

Poaching is an ever-present problem in the Great Glen. Lightweight, near-invisible nets, set just below the surface, take a terrible toll of returning fish. But the main culprits, in everyone's opinion, are the netters of salmon at sea. Every gillie to whom I spoke pleaded for action to curtail the never-ending slaughter.

Salmon fishing is Jock's greatest delight, despite his love of stalking. One of his earliest gentlemen was Major Waddington, angling author and inventor of the famous fly that bears his name. Jock fished with the Major in the days when he used to come regularly to the Garry. In spite of some friendly rivalry, there was a great degree of shared respect, although Jock regards fishing with anything other than traditional flies to be nothing short of heresy.

41

'I've a fancy for the old patterns: Thunder and Lightning, Silver Wilkinson and Hairy Mary, all lightly dressed. They've always been good friends to me.'

But the Major was willing to learn. One pool on the Garry is known as the Chest Pool, and Major Waddington complained that he had never caught a fish in it. One morning, standing above the Chest Pool, Jock asked the Major if he could see the fish. He couldn't, so Jock pointed them out, in a hollow, just on the edge of the main stream. The Major had been looking and fishing in the wrong place. Every day after that the Major took a fish from the pool.

Major Waddington claimed that a running fish would never take the fly. But on the Garry, they do.

'If you see a fish arriving in a pool and get your fly over him quickly enough, then he'll have it', Jock told me. 'But sometimes a fish will follow the fly and take it away from his normal lie, and that can fool an angler into wasting time fishing in the wrong place.'

Like all good gillies, Jock knows every lie on the river and was on hand to land the Major's best fish, a salmon of 36 lb taken from the Dog Pool. Jock claims that by the end of his days with Major Waddington, 'If I'd told him it might do, he'd have put the heel of his boot on and cast with it!'

Jock still has a book which Major Waddington inscribed: 'I hope you will learn as much from this little book of mine as I have learned from you over the years we have fished together.'

Like most of the old breed of stalkers and keepers, Jock can turn his hand to every aspect of estate work. Apart from stalking, fishing, vermin-control and the hundred-and-one other things a keeper is expected to do, he has also keepered the grouse moor. Grouse feed on heather that is three to four years old. Birds come down in early morning and spend the midday hours on their roosting grounds before returning to feed again in late evening. In hot summer months, when the hill may be scorched and dry, grouse take to the sides of burns and lochs, or shelter under bog-myrtle and bracken. When storms and gales threaten, they seek higher ground and the lee-sides of screes and corries.

Grouse shooting on the estate was all walking up, over dogs. Jock would go through his ground before The Twelfth and note the different coveys and the number of birds in them. Then he could quickly direct the gentlemen, giving them plenty of time to load before slipping the dog.

Jock worked mostly with pointers and had a favourite dog that could point a dead bird. Jock preferred pointers to setters because pointers have harder feet. Jock found that setters tended to get damp 'clobbers' round their legs and heather in between their toes. He found pointers to be much more clean-footed animals, and noticed over the years that a streamlined dog was being bred.

In times gone by, Jock explained, keepers used to soak their dog's feet in a strong brine solution at the beginning of the season to harden them, but if a dog was worked hard for an hour, then he had to be rested. Now one pointer can go almost the whole day through.

A keeper has to have as good a knowledge of the habits of his gentlemen as he has of the habits of his grouse, for never a season passes without a pointless accident.

Jock always warns his gentlemen that, on the hill, silence is golden. Of all the folk he has shot with, he claims that Frenchmen are the most difficult to control, 'Jabbering and squawking away like a gaggle of geese, scaring every damned bird for miles and as likely to shoot you as anything else. I'm sure some of them have never fired a gun before!'

He remembers one party of Frenchmen who were particularly difficult. No sooner had the dog gone in to flush than they started blasting away, and on several occasions they almost shot both dog and keeper. The retriever was having a terrible job bringing back shot birds, and when Jock looked he found the poor beast was trying to pick up a bundle of worthless feathers, loosely held together by broken wings. He had a boy with him who could speak French, so eventually he warned the guns that if they didn't behave properly, he'd put them off the hill.

As Jock said: 'That would never happen with an English or a Scottish gentleman, because they've been properly taught. People must be well trained, know how to handle a gun and how to behave on the hill. I remember one young lad coming in for lunch and his father asking him if he'd unloaded his gun. The boy replied that he'd forgotten. Well, his father made him walk the rest of the afternoon with an unloaded gun. He wasn't allowed to fire another shot all day. I was sorry for the boy, but his father was right. That's how accidents happen. People just mustn't forget such important rules.'

Night had crept up unnoticed as we sat talking in Jock's homely living-room. A cold March wind whistled through the trees along the river and Jock rose to put more peat on the fire. I produced a flask and filled two glasses. Jock sipped reflectively, the firelight sparkling in the straw-coloured 'water of life'.

'It minds me of Joycey Munro, in Perthshire. What a man for the drams!'

Joycey Munro was a keeper on the Dunalastair Estate, between Loch Tummel and Loch Rannoch, and his nickname was The Jacobite. He was full of tales of the days of Bonnie Prince Charlie and spoke as though he had been at the Prince's side from the moment he landed to the day he set sail for France.

Jock remembers that Joycey's love of a dram often had him in trouble. In those days, on a grouse drive, there were always more drams than enough for everyone. A certain amount was taken for the beaters, so much for the loaders, and, of course, the gentlemen had their own.

'Now, there was some that didn't want and some that didn't take', said Jock, 'and Joycey generally benefited from it all. Before long he was at the Gaelic and Bonnie Prince Charlie and could hardly see the moor, let alone walk over it. So, when he collapsed, we'd just find a hole, roll him into it and cover him with heather to keep the damp out. It would've been hard to see him getting into trouble. Jobs were hard to come by then. At the end of the day, when everything was being put away, and the Laird wasn't looking, we'd dig him up and help him home.'

One night, as he was being assisted home, Joycey turned on his helper and asked if he 'had' the Gaelic. The struggling unfortunate replied that although he had not a single word of Gaelic, he was every bit as Scottish as Joycey.

'Oh, you're like the wild cat. You're not in it!' said Joycey. He meant that, like the present-day wild cat, his friend had been so cross-bred that he had no right to call himself Scottish.

As Jock finished, I wondered how many Highlanders today would leave all and risk all to follow a modern Bonnie Prince Charlie? Romantic notions of the troubled times of the '45 Rebellion are so deeply entrenched in Scottish folklore that the stark reality of the disaster is forgotten.

Near to Jock's cottage, where we sat safely blethering, at Craig an Fhithich (The Rock of the Raven), are the ruins of Invergarry Castle, ancient home of the MacDonnells of Glengarry, burned by 'Butcher' Cumberland in 1748. People were hunted and killed like animals throughout the north of Scotland, yet still the romantic myths persist. A centuries-old tradition was destroyed; an ancient and proud race stripped of its possessions, dignity, and even its language. No, it was a sad, sad day when that French-speaking 'dandy' adventured into Caledonia.

Westwards up Glengarry, surrounded by Gairich (3,075 ft), Meall Coire nan Saobhaidh (2,695 ft), Sorn a'Choire Ghairbh (3,066 ft) and Ben Tee (2,957 ft) lie a series of excellent trout lochs: Loch Garry, Inchlaggan, Poulary and Quoich. Some of the largest brown trout ever caught have been taken here and I asked Jock about them. He told me of Mrs Grant's record-breaking brown trout, caught on 19th September 1957 in Loch Poulary and weighing 17lb 8oz. Mrs Grant was fly fishing for salmon at the time and the trout came to a small Jock Scot. After a considerable struggle, Mr Grant, who was acting as gillie at the time, gaffed the fish.

But to Jock, the newly created hydro-lochs, such as Loch Loyne and Cluanie, are 'big, black, dismal places'. He prefers the sparkle and surge of Oich and Garry salmon.

Although the Garry is some forty miles from the sea, salmon make the journey very quickly. Many of the fish caught, particularly spring salmon, have sea-lice on them. But not everyone believes that the sea-lice travel with the salmon. Jock told me that one evening, while laying out the day's catch in the hotel, a neighbour turned and said: 'Och, MacAskill, you have a little box of them in your pocket and sure but you don't just stick them on to the salmon before bringing them in for us to see.'

There was a twinkle in Jock's eye as he told me the story, and I thought to myself that there might just be a grain of truth in it.

He saw me to the door and we stood outside for a moment, listening to the river hurrying busily over the boulders and the sound of the storm rushing through the woods. I made my farewells and Jock directed me out. As I travelled back up the Great Glen, to Inverness, the road ahead shone with frost, and my mind shone with the memory of the pleasure of the company of one of nature's gentlemen.

CHAPTER 4

Tales from Tweedmill Cottage and Frank Binnie

Although I live in the far north of Scotland, amid the wild and empty moorlands of Caithness, a corner of my soul is forever 'Tweed'. It was on Tweed, more years ago than I care to remember, that I first committed the sin of angling—on Lyne Water, to be precise, a tributary of Tweed, near Peebles.

Unbeknown to me, that same year, a few miles upstream, a young lass was also taking her first, stumbling steps into the gentle art. Seven years later we met and married: Ann, my best companion, friend and fishing partner.

As a boy, I haunted the river, from Lyne Footbridge to Walkerburn Cauld. From ice-cold February until damp November's chills, I walked and fished, learning my lessons the hard way, by personal experience. Days seemed endless and a ½ lb trout a monster catch. Indeed, any catch at all made a red-letter day. With remarkable patience in one so young, I taught myself the essentials of angling: catching trees; retrieving casts from underwater obstructions; filling wellington boots with water; casting barbless flies; casting with no flies at all; falling in; and removing hooks from the back of my neck.

It was on Lyne Water that I had my first encounter with Tweed salmon. I was fishing near Lyne Station, where a Queen Victoria post-box was set into a cottage wall. At least it used to be, before the station closed. Darkness had fallen, and evening had merged into a gentle, all-enveloping May-night stillness, full of the scent of wild flowers and tumbling water. Bats flicked past, as by the light of a match—well, matches—I struggled to remove a Grouse and Claret from my jumper.

As I knelt in the long grass by the river, there was a sudden 'explosion'. The surface of the water shattered and sparkled as a great fish hurled itself clear, moonlight flashing along its silvery flanks. As if in slow motion, the shape hit the surface and the sound of its landing echoed through the quiet night. Waves from its spectacular leap rushed over the surface, sweeping into the bank at my feet. Birds rose startled from sleep and scattered through the trees.

I had never seen anything so magnificent, or experienced such heart-stopping excitement. It was as though the whole world stood still, as though a great secret had been revealed and shared. I knelt, motionless, until the river settled. From that moment, I became a confirmed angler, and I have remained so ever since.

When I had to leave Scotland, memories of those days sustained me: the thin line of pines on the crest of Wallace Hill near Innerleithen, pricking the pink and blue of evening; sunlight and shadows by the old bridge at Manor; ice-fringed margins at Cadrona; that unforgettable summer smell of nightfall on Tweed; and always, some- where in the gloaming, the swirl and splash of rising fish.

During service for Queen and Country, in the deserts of Southern Arabia, bumping over dusty, boulder-strewn mountain tracks, or mile after endless mile along sun- baked Indian Ocean shores, my thoughts turned constantly to that gentle valley, where sweet flows lovely Tweed. Even now, as the train thunders over the Border Bridge at Berwick, I know I'm really home.

Tweed, Queen of Scottish rivers, is famous for the huge salmon that surge upstream amid autumn's multi- coloured hues; for its broken runs and lazy summer pools where brown trout lie; for the mighty dash and sparkle of its silver spring salmon. It holds a lifetime's pleasure and contentment for the angler.

Tweed rises from the green Lowther Hills and flows eastwards, one hundred miles through Scotland's Border lands; through salmon beats synonymous with all that's best in fishing—Bemersyde, Mertoun, Makerstoun, Upper and Lower Floors, the world-famous Junction Pool, where Tweed meets Teviot, Hendersyde, Birgham and Tweedmill; past the grandeur of Sir Walter Scott's home at Abbotsford; Sprouston, where in May, 1854, Canon William Greenwell, of Durham, devised his matchless trout fly, the Greenwell's Glory, and sought the services of the incomparable James Wright to dress it; through the deep pool at Ladykirk, where James IV nearly drowned in 1500; gathering in waters from almost 2,000 square miles; hurrying past Lyne, Manor, Eddlestone, Lethien, Ettrick, Gala, Leader, Teviot, Eden, Leet, Till and Whiteadder to the North Sea.

On a cold afternoon in March last year, as I sped south down the A68 from Edinburgh, the 'auld grey city', my heart quickened again with the old sense of excitement: over Soutra Hill, following the route Bonnie Prince Charlie and his ragged band of Highlanders trudged on their way to Derby in 1745; across Fala Moor, where many a traveller has come to grief among the treacherous bogs and marshes; and then, the glory of the Eildon Hills, surrounded by well-tended, red-earthed Roxburgh fields.

In Kelso, I stayed at Ednam House Hotel, mecca for generations of salmon fishers, where the same air of eager anticipation prevailed, although different faces scrambled to be off in the morning. But one reminder of old days remained: the display of salmon flies in the bar; proper salmon flies, single-hooked and beautifully dressed. I had come to see the maker of these flies, Frank Binnie, one of the most knowledgeable and respected gillies ever to cast a line on Tweed.

Next morning, I drove eastwards from Kelso, through Birgham and Coldstream, following Tweed's north bank to Lennel; then right on the minor road and down the rough track leading to Frank's cottage at Tweedmill, looking across the river to Tillmouth in Northumberland.

A trim hedge enclosed a neat, well-tended garden in front of the house. I parked the car and, as the notice politely requested, shut the gate behind me. The front door was open and my knock was greeted by a cheery invitation to enter. Frank Binnie was seated by the fire, a black Labrador comfortably at his feet. The busy sound of pots and pans told me that Mrs Binnie was in the kitchen, preparing lunch.

The sitting-room was furnished in the old way: large well-polished table in the middle of the room, sideboard, display cabinet and armchairs. The Labrador rose lazily, tail wagging, and came over to nuzzle my hand.

Frank is a thick-set, young octogenerian. Because of arthritis, the gillie's occupational hazard, he retired a few years ago, but he still sees his old friends and gentlemen when they come to fish at Tweedmill. He was born at Innerleithen, near Peebles, and as a laddie used to 'puddle about for minnows and parr in Leithen Water'.

When he left school, Frank served his time as a grocer in Berwick, but barely a year had passed before the First

World War broke out. Like so many of his friends, Frank Binnie joined the army and served in Flanders and occupied Germany until 1919. He remembers the long wait for demob: 'If you were a pit man or a miner, you were quickly out, but an apprentice grocer had to wait a long time indeed.'

He returned to Berwick and the trade of grocer, in the employment of John Dodds. But Mr Dodds was also a keen angler and amateur naturalist, writing in the local paper and lecturing to the Berwick field club. So it was he who first took Frank fishing to Tweedmill, where he has stayed, working as a gillie, for more than seventy years.

A mill used to stand by the river. The remains of it are just upstream from Frank's cottage. The original structure was built in 1747, when a man named Gillespie started business there. But the great floods of 1831 broke the cauld and swept the mill away, and no sooner had repairs been carried out than another flood destroyed the work.

The cost of this disaster brought the business to bankruptcy, and the Gillespie family emigrated, working their passage to Australia. That was the last that was heard of them until 1932. Frank was working in his garden one morning when he noticed a man poking around among the ruins of the mill.

Eventually, the fellow came over and asked Frank if he could have the stone with the date '1747' inscribed on it. The visitor was a tall, well-built man of advancing years and, from his accent, Australian. He told Frank that his great-grandfather had been a tenant of the mill, and he wanted to take the stone back as a memorial to him.

Well, the Australian gentleman spoke to the Laird and was given permission to take the stone. But the Laird made him leave a replacement stone, and that one still stands there, bearing the inscription: 'This stone replaces the one bearing the date 1747, presented by the Laird to the firm of Gillespie Brothers of Australia.' The descendants of the disaster at Tweedmill had prospered in Australia and become the biggest mill-owners in the land.

The Binnies' cottage has been flooded three times over the years. On the last occasion, in 1948, the water reached half-way up the wall of the sitting-room. Frank, like most gillies, has a fine sense of history. He took a stone with the mark of the water clear on it, and sent it out to Gillespie Brothers in Australia, with a message saying: 'This is the likes of what sent your ancestor away to Australia—it's an ill-wind that doesn't blow somebody some good!' He never had any word back to say if the stone had arrived, so Frank deduced, with a fine sense of logic, that: 'They must be very funny people, Australians.'

Frank Binnie has gillied for hundreds of gentlemen, but he says that his greatest pleasure has come from teaching young folk to fish. All the McEwens of Marchmont started their angling days under Frank's benevolent gaze. Dr Fison, of Christchurch, caught his famous 53 lb salmon with Frank.

But times have changed, and not for the better: 'In the old days, if a gentleman got a salmon, he was delighted; and if he got two, he was overjoyed. Now, if they get ten, they want twenty; and if they get twenty, they want even more ... always wanting more. No more sportsmen are they than a sow's ear is a silk purse.'

One of the great characters who used to fish with Frank at Tweedmill was the author and naturalist, G. P. R. Balfour Kinnear. Their's was a tempestuous relationship, each regarding the other with a high degree of competitive respect. 'You know as much about it as my foot', Frank would say. 'All you've learned and put in your books has been gleaned from the likes of me, and very little thanks do we get for it.'

One morning Frank was pottering in the garden, keeping one eye on his vegetables and the other on Balfour Kinnear, who was fiddling about on the river-bank doing something to his line, which was laid out in the grass round his feet.

Unable to restrain his curiosity, Frank wandered over to see what was going on. 'What are you up to this morning, Mr Kinnear?' he enquired.

'You wouldn't understand, Frank, but I'm greasing my line. That's what I'm doing.'

'Greasing your line? Why would you be wanting to do a thing like that?' Frank asked.

He then received a long lecture on the merits of greased-line fishing for salmon, as recently demonstrated by Arthur Wood on the Aberdeenshire Dee, and was told of the great numbers of fish to be caught using this new method.

'Oh, is that so, Sir?' said Frank.

'You'll catch nothing today, Frank, unless you are fishing with a greased line, so be a good fellow and stop bothering me. I've fish to catch before lunch.'

Frank turned, walked back to the cottage in contemplative mood, and returned carrying his old greenheart salmon rod.

When Balfour Kinnear looked up and saw the rod, he stopped and asked Frank what he was going to do.

'Well, just to prove how little I know about fishing, and how wrong I am, I'll tell you what we'll do. I'll fish down the pool before you. You'll know perfectly well that I won't catch anything because my line's not greased. Then you come down behind me and catch three or four.'

But Balfour Kinnear would have none of it, and insisted that Frank fish down behind him.

'But that wouldn't be proving anything at all', explained Frank. 'Let me go down first, and when I don't catch anything and you do, then you'll see me greasing my line.'

Balfour Kinnear wouldn't agree, and Frank sat and watched as he fished down the pool, taking a grand salmon of 17 lb after the fourth cast. But Frank knew that if he had gone down first, the fish would have been his, and to this day he claims that Balfour Kinnear knew it just as well.

Late one summer evening there came an urgent knocking at Tweedmill Cottage door, and Frank found an agitated Mr Kinnear standing outside. He wanted help to take a photograph for the front cover of his new book, and it had to be done there and then. In spite of the fact that Frank had never before taken a photograph, Balfour Kinnear insisted that there was nothing to it. Unwillingly, Frank agreed to help.

The object of the exercise was to photograph Balfour Kinnear playing a salmon. Frank pointed out that, good fisherman though he was, Balfour Kinnear might wait all night and all the next day before hooking a fish. Wouldn't it be better if Frank did the fishing and Balfour Kinnear the photography?

Ignoring the thinly-veiled insult, Balfour Kinnear produced a 17 lb salmon, fresh from the freezer, and explained his 'master plan'. He would attach the fish firmly to a large tube-fly, throw it into the air over the river, and pick up his rod. Frank would take the picture just as the fish hit the water.

'And you think it will work, do you, Mr Kinnear?'

'Will you be serious, Frank? Let's get on with it.'

Basic instruction was given in the use of the camera and everything set ready. All Frank had to do was look through the view-finder and press the button at the right moment.

So the scene was set: a doubtful gillie, peering through the camera, and an optimistic author with the barely-defrosted salmon held aloft, in both hands.

'Ready, Frank?'

'Ready.'

Balfour Kinnear charged riverwards. Frank crouched, poised expectantly, finger on the button.

There came a great roar and a crash. Through the view-finder Frank saw Balfour Kinnear toppling backwards

54

into a clump of gorse, the salmon still firmly in his grasp—
so he took the shot. The weight of the salmon had overbalanced Balfour Kinnear. Had it not, then another yard
and both Balfour Kinnear and the fish would have been in
the river.

Hard though it was not to laugh, Frank managed
to keep a straight face, but that put an end to further
thoughts of photographic glory. Balfour Kinnear packed
up and left as soon as he had recovered his rod, salmon and
dented dignity.

Over the years Frank has seen many of the delightful
photographs taken by Balfour Kinnear. But there is one
he has never seen ... The incident was never mentioned
again, but Frank often muses upon what that photograph
would have looked like on the front cover of an 'expert's'
book on salmon-fishing!

Nevertheless, Frank always had a great respect and
affection for Balfour Kinnear, and claimed that the
gentleman didn't know the meaning of fear. He would
wade deeper than any other man Frank knew, and each
season he always had more fish than most.

Another exponent of greased-line fishing for salmon
was Lord Lochlagan, the Labour peer. He fished with
Frank one day more than thirty years ago and, as Frank
explained: 'He wasn't the sort of man to be told or argued
with, so I had a fine time of it.'

His Lordship arrived at the river and instructed Frank
to grease the line and put up a fly. He handed Frank a
small, rusty tin box containing three, old, chewed-up
Black Doctors. After the first cast from the boat, the line
sank and Lord Lochlagan accused Frank of greasing it
improperly.

'Here, Binnie! This line is not properly greased.'

'Well, if you think that, your Lordship, I'll just have to
row ashore and you can stand and watch me do it again.'

After Frank had regreased the line, Lord Lochlagan
complained again, but there was nothing wrong—other

than the fact that he didn't know how to fish it. Frank was instructed to get on to Dickson's in Edinburgh and have a new line sent down immediately.

'Do you want me to row ashore and do it now, or shall we wait until the end of the day?' enquired Frank.

'Don't be stupid, man! Do it later!' came the cross response.

After a while Frank saw a salmon following the boat and thought to himself: 'If that salmon isn't looking at the fly, then he very nearly is.'

The line stopped as the fish took the fly, turned, and began to go away. But Lord Lochlagan just sat there, doing nothing whatsoever about it.

'He's here, Binnie! He's here!' he whispered.

'I've known that for some time, My Lord!'

'What should I do?'

The line was taut by this time and moving slowly from side to side, so Frank told him that the natural thing to do would be to strike and get on with the business.

No sooner had he said that than up stood Lochlagan and, gripping the rod with both hands, gave an almighty yank. *Crack*! Sure enough, all that was left was a bit of gut, blowing in the wind. The disappointed peer turned to Frank and asked what had happened.

'Happened? I'll tell you. You're a very lucky man. If that gut hadn't broken, the fish coming flying past the boat could've knocked your brains clean out!'

The old gut casts were always difficult to handle and had to be well soaked in glycerine for several hours before use to make them supple. Frank carefully put up another cast, using the second of the ragged Black Doctors, then went downstream to a part of the river which he knew held no fish. But he didn't tell His Lordship. Instead he said: 'D'you see that yellow bush on the other side of the river, My Lord? Well, just cast towards it and we might be lucky.'

After a while, when the cast had straightened, Frank

took him back up to The Pot Pool. Within minutes another salmon was following the fly. This time Lord Lochlagan saw the fish, but he was still a little bit shaken by his last experience:

'He's here again, Binnie! What will I do?'

'For goodness sake don't do the same as you did last time! We've had quite enough of that. Just gie your wrist a bit twist and raise the point of the rod.'

Well, he did, and the salmon hooked itself. Half-an-hour later Frank had it safely in the boat, a fine fish of 10 lb, and the sea-lice still on him.

Lord Lochlagan took two more fish and by lunch was considering himself to be a real expert. Like any good gillie, Frank didn't disillusion him: 'The better they think they are, the harder they work!'

In the afternoon rain put the fish down, so, to give his gentleman as good a day as possible, Frank asked if His Lordship had such a thing as a spinning rod.

The rod produced was in the same condition as the fly-box—old, bent and uncared for.

'You surely don't use a thing like this for fishing, My Lord?'

'Why ever not? What d'you think I do with it?'

'Well, in this part of the world, we beat carpets with things like this!'

There was nothing for it but to try, so Frank put up the rod and mounted a lure. The sun shone and before long, sure enough, a salmon came chasing after the lure. His Lordship, staring into the heavens didn't see it, so Frank called out and pointed to the fish. Instead of giving the salmon a chance to take, Lord Lochlagan lifted the lure from the water and left the salmon, nose out, looking round for it.

'Drop the lure into the water, man! D'you expect the brute to dance for it?'

As soon as the lure touched the surface, the salmon had it and set off like an express train. But it didn't get very far, for the gentleman just sat there, keeping a tight hold on the line. He shouted at Frank to row after the fish and Frank shouted back to let the fish run. The rod was bent almost double, while Frank rowed like mad all round the pool, trying to keep pace with the enraged salmon:

'Row, Binnie! Row!' shouted the gentleman.

'For God's sake! Let it run, man!' Frank yelled back.

The situation reached such a state that Frank knew there could be only two possible outcomes: either he was going to collapse at the oars or the rod was going to break. In desperation, he threw down the oars and, as the salmon made a run alongside the boat, dashed the landing-net over the side. The salmon swam straight in and, with one mighty heave, Frank had it into the boat.

It then became clear why the gentleman wouldn't let the fish run. He couldn't. The spinning line was in a complete tangle and the reel was jammed solid:

'Do you see this line, My Lord?'

'Never mind, Binnie! I got the fish!'

'He' had got the fish!

Frank took a deep breath and replied, 'Well, so you did, My Lord! But you damn near gave me a heart attack in the process.'

That was enough excitement for the gentleman for one day, and Frank was more than ready to agree to finish. Ashore, the four fish were weighed, laid out and photographed. The sun shining on the salmon was as bright as the smile on His Lordship's face. An onlooker would have thought that it was all due to his own skill that four fish totalling 52lb were lying on the bank.

It was a happy gentleman who left Tweedmill that evening. But as Frank said: 'What is a gillie for if it isn't to send his gentleman off smiling?'

Mrs Binnie came through from the kitchen and, within moments, the table was spread with home-baking and a pot of tea. Mrs Binnie is a small, smiling, busy lady, well accustomed to dealing with her husband's stream of visitors and listening to their constant chatter and tall tales about fishing.

One of Frank's old fishing companions had called recently with such a story. He had been out with a gentleman on Loch Ness and soon realised that his gentleman knew little about the catching of salmon. But salmon often run the loch close to the north shore, ten to fifteen yards out from the bank. The gillie had put the gentleman over a good lie and a fish of about 20 lb had grabbed the fly. The man got such a fright that he fell over backwards, knocking the gillie from his seat.

The outboard motor came loose; the top section of the rod went into the loch; and the reel fell from the butt. And as if that were not enough, the strong wind was blowing them on to rocks above deep water. All this time, astern, ahead, round and under the boat, the salmon was dashing about like a mad thing, leaping and splashing.

The gillie eventually regained his seat, secured the outboard, calmed the gentleman, fixed the reel back in position, re-fitted the top section, brought the salmon under control and landed it—just before the boat ran on to the rocks.

With commendable presence of mind and patience, he turned to his gentleman and said: 'Well done, Sir! Played like a master!'

At that, a tremendous cheer broke out, accompanied by loud hand-clapping. They looked up to the road and saw that three buses and about five cars had stopped while the occupants watched their efforts, with cameras clicking, and waving and shouting their appreciation. Frank said his friend had never felt more foolish in all his life, but the gentleman stood bowing, doffing his hat, smiling and waving back, as happy as could be. He never for a moment realised that he had very nearly lost both the salmon and his life.

Anglers are not the only visitors to Tweed. As on most

of Scotland's salmon rivers, poachers play havoc with their netting and gassing of pools.

Poaching was rife even in my own early days on the Tweed, and, contrary to popular belief, nine times out of ten the locals were the greatest culprits. Worse, just one bailiff had to keeper several miles of river. His name was Fraser, a native of Aberdeen. He would cycle along the railway line, on an old bike and appear ghost-like through the bushes to ask for my permit. But he was a cheerful, happy man, always ready to stop and give a young lad good advice. I remember him with affection.

The locals at Innerleithen were a different kettle of fish. Even in the broad light of day they would work away, sniggering the pool below the bridge. In those days my Father and I used to park the car in the woods, across from the little cottage at the north end of the bridge. Father was always one for having a look first, and one morning, having tackled up, I glanced up from the river bank to see him standing studying the pool. On the far side, one of the locals was casting furiously and calling to Father, asking for directions to get his fly across a fish.

I knew exactly what the man was trying to achieve, but Father didn't, being not only short-sighted but also a trusting individual. Putting down my rod, I crossed the bridge to the perspiring fisherman. As I arrived, a particularly vigorous back-cast sent the fly into the branches of an old beech tree. I climbed up and released the fly. It was about five inches long, featherless and needle-sharp.

'What sort of fly do you call this?' I asked.

'That's what we call a Scott Jock, son. Now just hand it here and away and mind your own business.'

Today, however, poaching is reaching epidemic proportions. No longer is it just one for the pot. It's a van-load for market, and but one more factor in the sad story of ever-decreasing salmon stocks.

Although most of Frank's life has been spent at

Tweedmill, he has a good knowledge of the rest of Scotland. He has fished the Thurso River in my home county of Caithness, the Naver, Conon, Beauly and often the Spey, when his gentlemen took him north to gillie. He has a great love for brown trout fishing also, and has explored the wilds of the Hebrides, the difficult limestone lochs of Durness in north-west Sutherland and Lochs Cama, Veyatie, Borolan and Urigill, near Elphin.

But the great love of his life has been Tweed. In the old days the most successful fly on the river was the Brown Turkey, better known as a west of Scotland fly, on rivers such as the Annan and the Nith, and best with a 'mealy tip'. Frank scorns many of the tactics used today and considers spinning to be 'just a poacher's racket!' To him, fly-fishing is all.

In his early days, his gentleman used the huge Tweed rods—18 ft long and hard, hard work to use. 'I've seen them not long started before they'd be haudding their backs with pain', he told me. His own preference is for a 14 ft rod, and he uses it with the skill and artistry that comes only from a lifetime's experience.

Of all the strange tales I heard during my travels around Scotland, talking to keepers, stalkers and gillies, one of the hardest to believe was told me by Frank. During his years at Tweedmill he has caught many, many salmon, but three of them were caught without him having to lift a finger, cast a line or touch a rod. Each time the fish jumped straight into the boat!

The largest was a salmon of 12 lb, and it came hurtling in without warning, catching Frank full in the chest and knocking him from his seat. The only other occupant of the boat was Frank's Labrador, and the pair of them chased the fish round and round the bottom of the boat before Frank, lashing away with his priest, hitting fingers, dog's backside and woodwork, managed to subdue it. This has happened three times to Frank Binnie. All I could say to him was that I envied his secret!

Talking is thirsty work, so we shared a dram and blethered on as only anglers can: fish caught, folk known, places visited, old tales and memories—as fine a way to pass the time as ever man devised, apart from actually fishing!

Darkness was falling as I took my leave, carefully shutting the garden gate behind me. Mist floated over the frozen fields, the river shone deep silver, and the first hunting owls hooted by. I stopped at the top of the hill and looked back to the small cottage, its lights glowing yellow in the gathering dusk. Frank's parting words stuck in my mind:

'There are a lot of nice and kind people in the world you know, and I've been very lucky to meet so many of them.'

As I turned north, I felt that I had been very lucky, too.

CHAPTER 5

Ratheanach and the children of the mist

It was a winter day at Kinloch Rannoch. The road from Pitlochry had just been opened up after snow, and it had taken an hour's careful driving to reach the village. We bumped our way past Queen's View. It was not unamused Victoria who gave it its name, but a more earthy Scottish Queen, luckless Mary, who visited the rocky promontory overlooking Loch Tummel in 1564 and was captivated by the view.

Sunlight sparkled on Loch Rannoch, and graceful Schiehallion (3,547 ft) was etched against an incredibly blue sky. The position of Am Slios Min, 'the smooth slope', was marked on the first map of Great Britain by Claudius Ptolemy (AD 127–51), Egyptian astronomer. Sixteen centuries later another astronomer came to

Schiehallion. In 1774 Dr Nevile Maskelyne, Astronomer Royal, conducted his famous experiments there to determine the specific gravity and weight of planet Earth.

Here, almost at the heart of Scotland, we were surrounded by some of the most dramatic, wild and lonely hills in the north. Ben Alder (3,757 ft), where fugitive Prince Charles Edward Stewart hid in a cave for several weeks after the disaster of Culloden, towered to the north. Westwards stretched the great wilderness of Rannoch Moor, Ratheanach, 'the watery place', a desolate plateau, 1,000 ft above sea level and scattered with lochs and lochans, unchanged for a thousand years. Loch Laidon lay like a silver scar across the moor, hurrying the cold waters from Stob Ghabhar and Stob a'Choire Odhair in Glencoe through Rannoch and Tummel to the Tay and North Sea.

These are the lands of the outlawed Clan Gregor, 'the children of the mist'. In 1603 the Privy Council in Edinburgh passed an Act ordering 'the extermination of that wicked, unhappy race of lawless lymmaris, callit the MacGregour'. The men were hunted like animals; women were branded on the forehead; children were transported to camps in the Lowlands and Ireland to serve as cattle boys.

This is a land full of Scotland's saddest history, peopled by ancient ghosts, dark deeds and grim reminders of a turbulent past.

To the south of Loch Tummel, in the hills above Lick, is a small loch called Loch a'Chait. It lies at an altitude of 1,500 ft and one summer day, my wife, Ann, and I decided to walk up to fish it. I have never been refused permission to fish for trout anywhere in Scotland. All one has to do is ask, pay the necessary fee, if any, and most owners grant access.

We called at Lick House and spoke to Major Whitson, owner of the estate. He readily gave us permission to fish, saying we were the first folk for years who had had the courtesy to ask.

The sun shone brightly as we climbed through the trees and out on to the hill. It was a steep, tiring climb, and after an hour or so we stopped for a rest above a small corrie. Carefully making our way down to the valley floor, we started to cross. Ann was behind me, but half-way across I was startled to see her running by at full speed.

As she went she called to me: 'Quick, quick, run, get out of here.' She was ashen-faced and obviously in distress, so I ran after her, calling to her to stop to tell me what was wrong.

'Something terrible has happened here', she gasped. 'Women and children in danger. Get out, quick.' She ran on and took the cliff at the far side like a mountain goat.

All Ann could tell me, later, was that she suddenly sensed great danger, and that women and children were crying and in fear. So I made it my business to find out more about the hunting of the MacGregors, who lived along the shores of the loch.

The clansmen would often receive advance warning of the arrival of their persecutors. Women and children would be hurried into the hills to the safety of a remote corrie. There they hid until danger passed. But they were not always safe. Sometimes the hunters, having dealt with the men, would scour the hills, looking for the missing women and children. And sometimes they found them.

The corrie where Ann experienced her fear and shock was situated in such a position that it is possible that it was once used as a place of refuge, but that the unfortunate folk hiding there were discovered and harmed. Of all the black deeds that mar Scotland's story, surely the hunting and massacre of the MacGregors was one of the darkest.

But we had come this winter's day to Perthshire not to awaken old ghosts, but to speak to three keepers who between them spanned more than 100 years of experience in the hills. One was a 'youngster' of more than eighty; the second, a recently retired stalker; and the third, a mere middle-aged stripling.

John Fisher is now retired and lives in a small cottage in Glen Lyon, not far from MacGregor's Leap. He has spent all his life walking, stalking and fishing. Now, resting before a warm fire in the cluttered 'Aladdin's Cave' of his small sitting-room, I looked across at the weather-beaten face and sparkling eyes, full of humour and kindliness.

The mantle-shelf was lined with photographs: grim-faced, tweed-clad figures, staring aggressively and standing proudly behind twisted antlers of dead stags; a cluster of eager Labradors, alert, waiting for that first welcome command; a head-scarfed woman, sipping sherry on the hill.

In a corner of the room, among a stack of salmon and trout rods, stood an old gun; from the kitchen came the smell of good, honest Scotch broth, simmering on the stove.

'Do you still manage out, John?' I asked.

'Not as much as I'd like, and when I do it's the devil of a job that I have seeing anything. It's the eyes that begin to let you down, you know. As the years go by it's not so easy to spot the deer on the hill or the salmon lying in the pool.'

John Fisher was born on 31 December, 1903, and started gillieing when he was fourteen. He worked on his grandfather's farm at Tynayere, near General Wade's Lyon Bridge, and then as a gillie from the Fortingall Hotel.

In those days only people with money fished the Lyon. They arrived by train at Aberfeldy and travelled to Fortingall by pony-and-trap. Eight gillies worked from the hotel, and John's wages were 3s 6d a day, lunch, and a gill of whisky, which he always took home to his grandfather.

For every salmon in the river now, John told me, there were 100 then. Opening day, 15 January, usually produced more than twenty fish. Catching them wasn't the problem: it was carrying them all back to the hotel at the end of the day. There were no cars then.

Head gillie was John Stewart, who, because of his tall stature and love of a good dram, was known as the Scatten, the Scottish name for a heron.

John Fisher's first day as a gillie was with Mr Patterson, of Camps Coffee—the man who still figures on the label of the bottle, astride a camp-stool. The Scatten was ill, so John was told to act as gillie for the party. Mr Patterson had brought with him his twin daughters, pretty young girls about the same age as John.

Mr Patterson hooked a large fish and played it gamely for more than an hour. When the fish showed no sign of tiring, and Mr Patterson did, he asked John to feel in his pocket for a knife with which to cut the cast. John refused to do so, and after an enormous struggle, lasting nearly two hours, John successfully managed to land a fish of 28 lb.

John got up from his chair and produced a letter which he had received only that morning from Mrs Helen Coles Patterson, one of the twins who was with him that day:

'Dear John,

'I had hoped to write to you saying how much I had enjoyed meeting you last year at Grandtully when I came up with my son to fish, and now I hear that you have been celebrating your eightieth birthday. Congratulations! You are a fine chap!

'I well remember when you first gillied for us and my father caught the 28-pounder and he said to you: "Give me my knife, John", and you, good lad that you were, said, "No, Sir, I canna put my hand in your pocket."

'It was fine, and I can always see you that day. John Stewart was gillieing for us that holiday, but he was ill, so you came instead. I think it was your very first day ever gillieing, but you were a nice lad, and so nice you still are.

'I could have done with a lot of Glen Lyon since then.

I think I was a good horseman—in fact I know I was—and took a bit of following across country, too. I also did well at show-jumping. Now I do nothing except think of the old days.

'I am no longer able to drive a car and have to wait until some lady is kind enough to come and take me out. I wish you the very best for 1984. I am 1903, so I have beaten you! We will meet again sometime.

'Yours,

'Helen Coles Patterson'

John sat silently for a moment, looking out of the window to where snow-clad branches glistened and sparkled in the afternoon sun, as though re-living the long-past fight with the huge salmon and seeing again the young lassies excitedly watching the battle.

The Lyon still produces excellent sport, with good salmon taken each season. In recent years a young friend of John Fisher, John Nevin, an Edinburgh businessman, has taken the first salmon in three successive seasons, 1982, 1983 and 1984, battling through 4 ft snow-drifts and breaking ice to fish. The fish all weighed more than 15 lb, and the heaviest, in 1983, weighed 19 lb.

When John Fisher started work, the youngest gillie always got either the most difficult gentleman or the worst tipper, and John had more than his fair share of both. He arrived at the hotel one morning and heard that one of the guests was a non-smoker, tee-total and 'crusty' into the bargain.

John thought to himself, 'Aye, that'll be mine!'

Sure enough, the Scatten said: 'That's your man today, John.'

It was a bitter February day, with snow and sleet, and cold as cold could be. John's gentleman had little experience of handling a big rod in the ice-filled gale. They fished the Broom Pool in the morning and by dint of good luck and John's knowledge of where the fish lay, two fine salmon were on the bank by lunchtime. In the afternoon they fished Peter's Pool and took four more fish.

For a gentleman more accustomed to returning in the evening fishless, this was sport indeed. In gratitude he gave John a tip of £7 and half a salmon.

Back at the hotel John Stewart, the Scatten, enquired with mock civility: 'Well John, did you get a good tip the day, lad?'

'Not bad, £7 and a bit of fish.'

The Scat nearly had a heart attack, and the very next morning was off with the generous gentleman like a shot. But he caught no more fish, tipped very little, and complained all week, asking for the return of 'that very good young man'.

Peter Dewar, of the Perth whisky distillers, named Peter's Pool, the pool below John's farm at Tynayere. John gillied for him for many years. Dewar caught a lot of salmon in Peter's Pool, the first when he was ten, just above the point of the pool. After a lash at the salmon, John found the gaff caught in the line, and away went the fish. 'But I had expected the fly to be in the salmon's mouth, not in its ruddy back!'

The most difficult gentlemen to work with, in John's opinion, were army officers. He complained that they would never listen to advice and treated the gillie as though he were a private soldier on a misdemeanour charge. If they caught anything, then it was all due to their expert ability; and if they caught nothing, then it was all due to the gillie's lack of experience.

But most of John's gentlemen over the years have been friends as well as guests. He still proudly wears a watch given him by Mr Booth, a gentleman he saved from drowning in Suspension Bridge Pool. The water was high and Mr Booth overbalanced. John, who doesn't swim, managed to gaff Mr Booth through his body-waders as he was being swept away and dragged him to the shore. Fortunately, the gentleman was a small man or the story might have had a very different end, strong though John Fisher was.

For two days each week, over a period of fifteen years, John gillied on the Grandtully beat of the Tay. It was there that he landed his biggest salmon, a fish of 42 lb. There was some rivalry between John Fisher and the head gillie on the beat, Kirby. When the fish was weighed, John claimed 42 lb, but Kirby would allow only 41 lb. 'That Kirby should have been bloody hunted for weighing my big fish wrong!'

Over the years John has caught almost every weight of salmon, from grilse right up to the big Grandtully fish. The only weight he has missed is 39 lb, but he told me there was still plenty of time to put that right.

Looking over at the bright face and twinkling eyes, I had no doubt that could well be so.

'Now, Bruce, you've listened to my blethers long enough. We'll have a wee something to warm us, and then I'll give you the finest bowl of soup in all Perthshire.'

He did, and it was.

Glen Lyon has more than just excellent salmon fishing. A walk up the glen is a walk through history. At Fortingall is the oldest tree in Europe, a 3,000-year-old yew in the churchyard. Pontius Pilate is reputed to have been born near Fortingall, 'the fort of the strangers'.

Further into the glen are the remains of the forts of Fionn, King of Scotland in the third century AD:

> *Twelve castles had Fionn,*
> *In the crooked glen of the stones.*

In the seventh century, Eonan, a priest from Iona, brought Christianity to Glen Lyon; and when the Black Death was advancing up the glen, Eonan, through prayer and devotion, halted its progress where the Allt Bail a'Mhuilinn burn enters the Lyon. The parishioners were somewhat less fortunate in the fourteenth century, when plague claimed the life of every inhabitant. A great stone in a roadside field marks their resting place.

Other less murderous visitors have been captivated by the glen. William Wordsworth and his sister, Dorothy, knew the area. Alfred Lord Tennyson, Poet Laureate, found comfort and inspiration on the tree-clad river-banks. The great Liberal Prime Minister, William Gladstone, often stayed there. Baden Powell, hero of Mafeking and founder of the Boy Scout movement, tried his fishing skill in the fast-flowing waters.

John Fisher gillied for Baden Powell when he made that visit to the Lyon. He remembers him as a quiet, reserved man and a good caster. But his principal memory of the Chief Scout is of the way in which he was closely mufflered against the biting wind.

Most of the land around Fortingall was owned by Sir Donald Currie. The shooting was not let out, but was used by Sir Donald's friends.

After leaving the warmth of John Fisher's cottage up the glen, I drove back towards Fortingall and stopped to meet David Dow, who worked as a keeper on the estate for twenty-two years.

David is a sparse man, wiry, quiet and with a gentle sense of humour. When he started work he was paid thirty-shillings a week and given a suit of clothes. He worked first on the Logiealmond Estate, then Rossie Priory and, latterly, Fortingall.

The keepers always have plenty of work on a mixed sporting estate. At Fortingall, the fishing starts on 15 January; the hill ground has to be prepared for the stalking and grouse; and 200 pheasants have to be reared.

But the sport is not nearly as good as it used to be because estates have insufficient keepers. Few landowners nowadays can afford to employ enough men to cope with all the tasks demanding attention. Vermin quickly get out of hand. A vixen will take more than ten young grouse in a morning to feed her litter. Sport suffers accordingly unless something is done.

David's main pleasure was stalking, and he had the reputation of being a man who never tired, but who could go on and on, effortlessly, hour after hour, all day. As a young man, he was known to run from Schiehallion to Fortingall, a distance of eight miles across rough, broken country, for fun.

David always gave his gentlemen a shot at the practice target before taking them on to the hill. This put them at their ease and avoided rifle shake, 'stag fever', before they shot in earnest.

To take two or three stags in a day is considered good sport, 'but it all depends on the conditions, wind and such like', David told me. 'In good weather the stags sit right on the tops and are difficult to get at. You just have to edge forward, an inch at a time. So many eyes are against you—hundreds of eyes, all watching, and they pick up the slightest movement. And you daren't move again until they've decided there's nothing to worry about.'

Stalking is in David's blood. His father, a keeper all his life, was in the employ of the Atholl Estates, and David, too, never wanted anything other than an outdoor life.

I called at the Fortingall Hotel to share a dram with Heather and Arthur Howard, and to thank them for arranging my meetings with John Fisher and David Dow. Then, with the light gone and frost covering the roads, I made my way carefully back over the hills to Kinloch Rannoch and the comfort of the Loch Rannoch Hotel.

The following morning I had the pleasure of meeting Peter Smith, who has worked as a keeper all over Scotland, from the Dufftown Estate to Aberfoyle. He went to the Glenlyon Estate as a young man of nineteen as under-keeper, but moved about over the years, gaining experience in most aspects of estate work and keepering.

He believes a keeper's job is to upset the balance of nature in such a fashion that you have more game than predators; to reduce the level of vermin and increase the stocks of grouse. The more successful a keeper is, the harder it becomes to keep down foxes, wild-cats and other natural predators.

But nowadays, to balance the books, estates show an increasing tendency to shoot into the stock of grouse: to take out more than the birds can naturally replace. If a 10,000-acre grouse moor is left holding only 100 pairs of birds at the end of the season, nothing is going to make them produce more than four or five eggs each, and sooner rather than later the sport will be worthless.

Peter has always preferred the challenge of stalking to that of other field sports, and over the years he has had many memorable days on the hill. I asked him who was the worst shot he had taken out. He replied unhesitatingly: 'Mr Abbott, from Glasgow.'

Most gentlemen today use telescopic sights, but a few still shoot over open sights. Mr Abbott, 6 ft tall, red-faced, with voice and tweeds to match, appeared one morning clutching an old four-shot Martini-Henry rifle. It was a beautiful gun, invented by an Austrian, Fredrich Martini, who sold the idea to the British Army in 1871.

'As far as Mr Abbott was concerned, for all he knew about it, he would have been better off using a bow-and-arrow. I think he must have spent a lot of time overseas. He treated me as though I had just emerged from a grass hut.

' "Now Peter", he explained, "I'm a little short-sighted, so I've brought my Martini-Henry with me today. So it will be all over open sights. Is that all right with you?"

' "Now, Mr Abbott, it's so many years since I fired over open sights that I'd hardly know where to look, let alone hit anything. But you're the one who's doing the shooting, so I've no objection at all."

'I took Mr Abbott down to the practice target and he fired off a couple of shots. Both missed. I decided there and then that he was more blind than short-sighted. Either that or he'd never handled a gun before, because we were firing from little more than sixty yards.

'I thought to myself that unless I brought the gentleman close enough to stroke the beasts, then, Martini-Henry or not, the stags on the hill could all rest peacefully that day.

'Well, we walked and crawled and stalked the whole day through. Every time I brought him in close enough, sure as anything, he would loose off a few rounds and the stags were none the wiser.

'Worse, hour after hour, I had to listen to a constant stream of stories and tales, all concerning Mr Abbott's great exploits on the hill. By evening, I was cold, wet, hungry, angry and ready to strangle the man should he so much as mention one more stag that he'd shot or one more country he'd visited!

'Towards evening I brought him in to a single stag, lying in a peat-hag about 300 ft below us. "Now, then, Sir", I said, "this will be the last chance you'll have today, so let's rest here awhile before going down. But when we do, be sure to follow close and keep very quiet, or the beast will surely see us and that'll be an end to it."

'Mr Abbott turned to me and laughed. "No chance of my being seen, Peter, not behind the great tackety boots you're wearing!"

'As if I hadn't been tortured enough all day! Now he was giving me lessons on boots!

' "Let me tell you, Mr Abbott, that these boots are made from the finest horse-hair and come all the way from Mr Rodgerson in Galashiels—and he makes the best stalking boots in the world."

' "You keep crawling, Peter. I'll keep hiding!"

'I set off on my belly, down this damp gully, Mr Abbott following on. But the stag wasn't caring. As we edged closer, I saw the beast was fast asleep. I stopped about eighty yards from the stag and got Mr Abbott into a comfortable position, telling him to take his time and to make sure that the first shot was the last.

'He grabbed the rifle and, almost without hesitation, loosed off a round. The bullet hit the peat-hag about six yards to the right of the stag. The beast slumbered on, uncaring. The second shot sent chips flying from a granite boulder to the left.

'Now the stag stood up and had a wee bit look around to see what was going on. It was standing broadside on and just a perfect target. Mr Abbott's third shot whined over the antlers and the beast decided that it had had enough of all this lead flying round.

'It sprang off, going fast, behind a huge rock. "Here you are, Peter", called Mr Abbott, throwing me the rifle. "Finish him off!"

' "Finish him off, be damned", I thought. "The beast hasn't been touched!" With one shot left, I threw the rifle to my shoulder and, with a shock, found myself staring down open sights for the first time in nearly twenty years.

'The stag came bursting from cover, flying like the wind, head high. I let the last bullet go and saw the beast go tippling head-over-heels into the heather. It was a fine stag, near fifteen stone.

' "Well done, Peter! Lucky shot!" said my gentleman.

'He was the worst shot I've ever known, and I've no doubt whatsoever that to this day, in club, lodge or bar, he tells anyone daft enough to listen the story of the flying stag taken cleanly between ear and eye with a single, well-aimed snap-shot from his trusty old Martini-Henry rifle.'

I could well imagine the type of man Peter had described. Such men are to be found throughout Scotland, lurking after dinner, voice-box primed and waiting to pounce on the unwary, weak and unsuspecting. Later that evening, in the hotel lounge bar, we looked carefully around before deciding that it was safe to go in. But perhaps Peter had been there first, Martini-Henry at the ready, just to make certain.

CHAPTER 6

Chess and chestwaders
on Spey and Dee

When I returned from Southern Arabia in 1960, the thought uppermost in my mind was of fishing. After nearly five years in foreign parts—that is, anywhere south of Tweed—I was as excited as a small boy with a pocket-full of money in a sweet shop.

I had enjoyed service for Queen and country, but, apart from two glorious weeks in Kenya, fishing the Rupengazi, of fishing there had been none. So I asked my father to join me for a fishing holiday on the Spey at Craigellachie.

We set off from Edinburgh full of hope and faith, entirely lacking any sense of charity towards the unsuspecting fish. Three, hard, fruitless days brought us back to reality:

the river was too low, the temperature too high, and throughout the week only one fish was caught. Even worse, two retired Generals were staying at the hotel and, as a newly-retired very junior officer, I was greatly intimidated by their presence.

In the evenings, after dinner, one of the Generals used to sit with *The Scotsman* newspaper. It was almost impossible to determine whether he was asleep or awake. His eyes seemed to be neither open nor shut, and from time to time his hands jerked convulsively, as though he was re-arranging the paper.

But the Generals were in fact quite human. One evening, after yet another hot, fishless day, I found one of them struggling to pull off his waders. So I gave him a hand. It was either that or watch him die of a heart attack, and even I was not as anti-establishment as that.

The General had caught a salmon, a modest beast of about 9 lb, and he kindly gave me the killer fly. In spite of all my efforts, however, the salmon refused to budge. Not so, however, a superb brown trout—in fact, the largest trout I had ever caught. One evening, salmon-less and in despair, I cursed and headed hotel and barwards as fast as I could go.

As I walked along the river-bank, I crossly flicked the line over the water. When the fish took, the rod was almost wrenched from my hand and I nearly died of fright. After what seemed a great struggle, I landed a trout of more than 3 lb. It was little enough reward for a week's salmon fishing, but was I pleased to see the fish safely on the bank.

The Spey is a perfect river: fast-flowing and surrounded by some of the finest scenery in all of Scotland. As a Boy Scout, my first venture away from home was to camp at Newtonmore, in 1950. Even then, in spite of dreadful weather, the magic of Speyside cast its spell, and I have remained enthralled ever since.

In the days before Aviemore became an inland Blackpool, my wife, Ann, spent holidays near Carrbridge. A happy gaggle of young folk used to set off on cycles, ride to Loch Morlich and then spend the day walking in the Cairngorms.

I always remember the sense of shock I felt on seeing a photograph of a 2 lb trout that Ann had caught high up in the Lairig Ghru. There was no denying its size. It had been photographed alongside a ruler. Until that moment I had felt secure and superior with regard to fishing. Over the ensuing twenty-five years I have learned otherwise. If fish are about, then Ann will catch not just one, but several, and always the largest. It is a sobering thought.

Our first visit to Speyside as a family was in 1963. For some reason it involved driving from Corfe Castle, in Dorset, right up to Nethy Bridge, where we had booked a cottage. Our life seems to have been full of huge expeditions caused by tangled arrangements and unhappy planning.

The river was in spate for the first part of the week, so we had no chance of a salmon, let alone trout. Nevertheless, when my back was turned, Ann shot off to worm a little tributary, and when I eventually caught up with her, gesticulating and remonstrating, she had a lovely fish of about 1 lb 8 oz on the bank.

For years we have had a running argument about fishing methods. Although Ann would never dream of using a worm in a loch, she reckons that a small stream in spate is fair game. That's the way it has always been, and, I have no doubt, always will be.

It was during that holiday that we first fished Lochindorb, to the north of Grantown-on-Spey. Lochindorb was, and still is, full of small trout, the ideal place for a beginner. Our day was windy and wild, but we still managed to catch more than a dozen little trout.

The most dramatic aspect of Lochindorb is the ruined castle on the island off the east shore. This was a lair of the infamous Wolf of Badenoch, Alexander Stewart, illegitimate son of King Robert II of Scotland. Deep in the bowels of the ruined castle are the remains of the water dungeon. Prisoners were cast into a cell full of water, the level of which reached their chests, and were left to stand, swim or sink. In 1390 the Wolf was excommunicated by the Bishop of Moray and, in return, sacked and burned the town of Forres and Elgin Cathedral.

The Spey has always been one of the foremost salmon rivers in Scotland, and although fishing is but a shadow of what it was in times past, great sport may still be had. One of the most famous stories of Spey salmon fishing is recounted by Thomas Tod Stoddart and tells of a huge fish hooked many years ago by one Duncan Grant.

'First you must understand that what is called "preserving the river" was formerly unknown, and everyone who chose to take a cast did so without let or hindrance.

'In pursuance of this custom, in the month of July, some thirty years ago, one Duncan Grant, a shoemaker by profession, who was more addicted to fishing than to his craft, went up the way from the village of Aberlour, in the north, to take a cast in some of the pools above Elchies-water. He had no great choice of tackle, as may be conceived; nothing, in fact, but what was useful, and scant supply of that.

'Duncan tried one or two pools without success, till he arrived at a very deep and rapid stream, facetiously termed the Mountebank. Here he paused, as if meditating whether he should throw his line or not. "She is very big", said he to himself, "but I'll try her; if I grip him he'll be worth the hauding."

'He then fished it, a step and a throw, about half-way down, when a heavy splash proclaimed that he had raised him, though he missed the fly. Going back a few paces, he came over him again, and hooked him.

'The first tug verified to Duncan his prognostication, that if he was there "he would be worth the hauding"; and he held fast, nothing daunted. Give and take went on with dubious advantage, the fish occasionally sulking.

'The thing at length became serious; and after a

succession of the same tactics, Duncan found himself at the Boat of Aberlour, seven hours after he had hooked his fish, the said fish fast under a stone, and himself completely tired. He had some thoughts of breaking his tackle and giving the thing up; but he finally hit upon an expedient to rest himself, and at the same time guard against the surprise and consequence of a sudden movement of the fish.

'He laid himself down comfortably on the banks, the butt end of his rod in front; and most ingeniously drew out part of his line, which he held in his teeth. "If he tugs when I'm sleeping", said he, "I think I'll find him noo"; and no doubt it is probable that he would.

'Accordingly, after a comfortable nap of three or four hours, Duncan was awoke by the most unceremonious tug at his jaws. In a moment he was on his feet, his rod well up, and the fish swattering down the stream. He followed as best he could, and was beginning to think of the rock at Craigellachie, when he found to his great relief that he could "get a pull on him". He had now comparatively easy work; and exactly twelve hours after hooking him, he clicked him at the head of Lord Fife's water: he weighed fifty-four pounds, Dutch, and had the tide-lice upon him.'

Big fish are still caught on the Spey and few have had more experience of catching them than Jimmy Ross, of Rothes. I called to see Jimmy one morning last March, when he kindly gave up a day's fishing to meet me. Most men of more than 80 would be content to sit by the fire and reminisce. Not so Jimmy Ross. He is as active as ever, fishing and shooting.

The day before I arrived he had been on the river with Major Ashley Cooper, and because it was so cold, he had started to light the fire in the fishing hut.

'Come on now, Jimmy. Never mind the fire. Let's get started', said the Major.

'Well', Jimmy thought to himself, 'I've been out in the

cold all my life and I'm quite used to it,' so he put up the tackle and off they went to the river.

'Right, Major', said Jimmy. 'Off you go and I'll follow you down.'

'No, Jimmy', replied the Major. 'Off you go and I'll follow you down.'

'That would never do!' said Jimmy.

'How long have we been fishing together, Jimmy?'

'As near enough twenty years as makes no difference.'

'Well, you will damned well go down first today and no argument!'

Jimmy did and was rewarded with a lovely 18 lb salmon, 'which the Major landed, just perfectly.'

Jimmy Ross was brought up on the Aberdeenshire Dee, where his father was a farmer. He was introduced to fishing by an old gillie at Aboyne: 'He gie me a bit gut and a fly and taught me all the knots I know or have ever used.'

The other Aboyne gillies, John Ingram, Billy Andrews and Willie Reid, told him about salmon-fishing, but Jimmy has spent most of his working life, forty-eight years so far, on his beloved Spey.

During his time on the Dee, Jimmy knew the famous Arthur Wood, at Cairnton, when all the talk was of greased-line fishing and the great havoc he was wreaking among the salmon with a small Blue Charm.

'Well, I knew his gillie and I used to see him in the pub at nights, so I asked him about all the fish being killed on a wee Blue Charm. "Don't you believe it", he said.

' "It's a great big Jock Scott that's doing all the work: and everybody for miles around lashing away with these little Blue Charms they've been reading about in the newspaper articles." '

Like many of his colleagues, Jimmy never learned to swim, and this oversight almost cost him his life one cold March day on the Dee. He had waded out just that little bit further than he should, and before he knew what had happened, he had been swept off his feet. However, an older keeper, Mr Grant, had warned the young man what to do in such an emergency, so Jimmy kept calm and just let the current carry him downstream.

After what seemed an age he managed to grip a large rock and pull himself up on to it. From this precarious perch, he shouted and bawled until he was blue in the face, but nobody heard. Cold, wet and frightened, he managed to hook a stout stick being swept by and, taking courage in both hands, waded the river, arriving safely on the Glen Tanar side, wet but wiser.

The Dee sometimes has flash floods. Jimmy remembers fishing with a gentleman one day when a huge wall of water suddenly appeared, rushing towards his angler. Jimmy shouted a warning, but the gentleman didn't understand: 'Get out man, get out! The water's coming down on you!'

'What are you saying, Jimmy? What's wrong?'

Jimmy arrived at the bank just as the wall hit the gentleman, and had it not been for the fact that he had a long, strong gaff, his gentleman would surely have drowned.

The diminishing quality of salmon-fishing on Spey is a cause for great concern to all anglers. Jimmy is firmly convinced, as am I, that the main culprit is netting at the river mouth and in the sea.

'Oh, bless my soul, when I think of the numbers of salmon we used to catch down here at Delfur in the old days! Some days, with Sir Edward Martin, we would have forty to fifty salmon. I remember one morning with Sir Edward when we had more than two dozen before lunch.'

The best day brought a total of 67 salmon, but the fishing was less commercial in those days. Most of the salmon caught were sent to local hospitals. Indeed, some gentlemen used to dispatch their fish to hospitals all the way down into England. But as Major Ashley Cooper often says to Jimmy: 'You and I have seen the best of it, Jimmy, you and I have seen the best!'

1   *Willie Hanton senior (page 182)*

2   *Willie Ross of Altnaharra*
(page 121)

3   *A final throw on the Spey at Blacksboat Bridge*

4 *'Roping down' on the Tweed at Sprouston Dub*

5 *Setting off with William Calder on the fateful expedition (page 147)*

6 'Matting' salmon for dispatch at Oykel Bridge, Ross-shire

7 The laird, Captain Alwyne Farquharson, fishing the Aberdeenshire Dee
with his head-keeper Donald MacDonald

8 *An anxious moment as the gillie nets his gentleman's fish on the Tweed*

9 *How it is done–Colin Leslie at Cargill beat on the Tay (page 143)*

10 *Watching hinds on the crest of a hill on the Arnisdale estate*

11 *Waiting for the call beside Loch Hourn, Inverness-shire*

12 'Glassing' the hills from a position high above Arnisdale Forest

13 Grouse shooting on the Isle of Arran — the gillie and his retriever standing
prudently behind

14 *Profiles of a partnership – gillie and gentleman spying on the hill*

15 *The long walk home*

16   Line up on the Invercauld estate: (left to right) Willie Bain, Roy Davidson, Colin McKintosh, James Davidson, Captain Farquharson (Laird), Donald MacDonald, Donald Campbell, Peter Fraser and Ronnie Hepburn

17   Richard McNicol and the author share a dram after hill loch fishing in Caithness

The largest salmon Jimmy has landed was a fish of 41 lb 8 oz for Mr Ronnie Faulkner. It was hooked in Dewsies Hole and eventually landed away down at Green Bank, by Croft's Farm. There was a ridge out in the Green Bank at that time and Jimmy had seen the dorsal fin of the salmon showing above the water. When he gaffed the fish, he was almost pulled into the river, and he had to kill the fish before he could haul it to the bank.

When Jimmy looked round to congratulate his gentle-man, Mr Faulkner was nowhere to be seen. His gentleman, in the excitement of playing the fish, had suffered a heart attack. The Land-Rover was some distance away, so Jimmy had to struggle home carrying both angler and fish.

The telephone rang, and Jimmy got up to answer it. He was busy for a few minutes arranging to go pigeon-shooting with a farmer friend, so I busied myself with hip-flask and two glasses.

'Would you care for a dram, Jimmy?' I said when he sat down.

'Well, it's never done me any harm. Thank you very much ... Here's to your good health and success with your stories.'

One of the stories Jimmy told me concerned the gaffing of a fish for the Duke of Beaufort—or not, as it turned out to be. Jimmy was sitting on the bank with the other gentlemen when he saw the Duke hooked into small fish. Jimmy poled the boat over the river and asked the Duke for his gaff.

The gaff was combined with a wading-staff, made by Hardy Brothers, with a spring on top to cover the point of the gaff. But Jimmy saw no need to take the spring off because the salmon was still in the middle of the river.

The Duke had little or no strain on the fish and Jimmy was convinced that the salmon had no idea that it had been hooked. There they both were: the Duke on the bank, the salmon in the middle of the river. Eventually, the salmon decided to have a swim round and, as luck would have it, came to rest about ten yards from where the Duke stood.

The Duke roared at Jimmy: 'What are you standing there for! Get in and get it man! Get in and get it! Good God, man! You haven't even got the gaff ready! What do you think you're playing at?'

But the fish was still in deep water, so Jimmy held his piece and stayed on the bank.

The Duke was red with anger and shouted at Jimmy: 'Will you get that fish when I tell you?'

So Jimmy unsprung the gaff, hooked it over the line, grabbed the line, pulled the fish in and killed it. He threw the fly to the gentleman, the fish in the boat, and poled back across the river.

That night, Jimmy told his good lady to start packing: 'That's it, dear! I've had a terrible row with the Duke today and I am thinking tomorrow we'll be leaving.'

But not another word was said, and Jimmy had no regrets: 'No one should speak to another man like that. It was only right that he should be shown how to land a little salmon without all that great fuss.'

Jimmy Ross is one of the most delightful men I have ever had the pleasure of meeting. Even after a lifetime's salmon-fishing on the Spey, his eyes still sparkle with all the brightness of a boy playing his first fish.

During my travels round Scotland, meeting gillies and keepers, collecting material for this book, I never thought that I would find myself fighting for my life near Grantown-on-Spey. My opponent was Jock Walker, and as the battle progressed, I realised I was going to be on the losing side.

It had all started when Jock asked if I could play chess. Foolishly, I said I could, and shortly afterwards I found myself on the receiving end of a short, sharp lesson in tactics.

Jock Walker came to the Seafield Estate in 1948, and he has worked as a gillie on the Spey ever since. Although Jock never really planned to be a gillie, he has enjoyed his time on the river and has met a host of characters over the years.

Salmon-fishing was not highly valued when Jock started with the estate, and the gillies did most of the fishing and caught most of the salmon. The old Spey salmon was a long, lean fish, but the quality of fish was greatly improved by the introduction of stock from the Inverness-shire Garry.

Although the estate water has four boats, most of the pools can be fished easily from the bank, which is much more fun in Jock's opinion.

Fortunately, Jock is not so ruthless with his fishing gentlemen as he was with me at chess. He has endless patience and over the years has introduced many visitors, both young and old, to the delights of salmon-fishing.

One day Jock was fishing with an American gentleman, whom he described as 'Not really the cleverest of anglers, more accustomed to his little spinning rod than a proper salmon rod.'

Given a beginner, Jock puts him where he is unlikely to catch fish, so that basic instruction in casting can be given without interruption. On this occasion the American gentleman sat dangling his fly above the water.

'Now then, Sir. Do you not think it would be a good idea to put your fly into the water so that the fish might be able to see it better?' said Jock.

The gentleman lowered the point of the rod and the fly sank below the surface.

'Now, Sir, if you were to cast the fly out to your left, the movement of the fly in the current might just attract a salmon.'

After a couple of hours, Jock had his gentleman casting reasonably well, so he took him to the top of the pool where, almost immediately, he hooked a good spring fish of about 12 lb.

The gentleman had such a shock that nearly all the line was off the reel before the fish stopped. He sat on the fishing stool, wide-eyed with astonishment and clinging to the rod like grim death, knuckles white with the strain. When Jock netted the fish, the American gentleman was so pleased with himself you would have thought he had caught the Crown Jewels. From that moment on he has been one of the keenest fly-fishers Jock has known.

The following day, Jock took his gentleman to Beat 3 and set him fishing from the bank. After a while Jock heard him swearing and cursing, pulling and heaving at the rod. The fly was snagged on the bottom. Before Jock could intervene, the cast broke and everything came flying back to land about the unhappy angler's ears.

'Are you all right, Sir?' enquired Jock.

'Damn it, Jock. I've been playing that fish for about 40 minutes, but I guess he's chewed the bug off my bit of string!'

Jock commiserated with his gentleman, but encouraged him to keep on trying. By the end of the week the American had managed to land twelve good salmon, and he left the Spey happy in the knowledge that he had 'mastered' the art of salmon-fishing!

Another American, a lady, fishing the Spey for the first time, caused Jock some amusement.

'Now, Madam, are you not supposed to cast the fly in front of you, rather than let it trail from the back of the boat?' asked Jock.

'Oh, really, are you? Back home in the States we always use a lead weight and a spinning reel. Don't you do that here?'

'No, Madam, we do not!' Jock answered firmly.

'Say, Jack', his lady enquired. 'Does the river always flow this way?'

'Well, Madam, it has done so for as long as I can remember.'

'But what happens when the tide comes in?'

'Now, Madam, since we are a good forty miles from the sea, I don't think the tide will be bothering us today!'

In spite of his best efforts, Jock could not put the lady into a fish. So on her last day he decided that he would have to do it for her. Jock took her to a spot where there was always a fish, behind a boulder on the far side:

'Now, Lady, I'll just get the first cast out for you.'

Jock placed the fly, to the inch, and by the time he had handed the rod to the lady, the salmon was firmly attached to the end.

'So the lady went back to the States well pleased with me and even better pleased with herself!'

Jock smiled as I surrendered my King.

'Another game?'

'If you catch salmon as well as you caught my Queen, I'd be willing to have lessons for as long as you like. Thanks for the game, and even more so for your tales!'

Bloody but unbowed, I retreated into the gathering gloom of a Speyside storm and headed eastwards to Ballater and Royal Deeside.

Although I have travelled extensively throughout Scotland, Deeside is an area that I have always seemed to miss. So it was with pleasure and excitement that I found myself at last by the clear waters of one of Scotland's most famous salmon rivers, flanked by tree-clad hills and mountains.

This is stalking and shooting country also, and I had come to meet three men who, between them, spanned more than seventy years' experience of sport on Deeside: Donald MacDonald, of Ballater; Tom MacPhearson, at Inchmarnoch; and Jimmy Oswald, present head-keeper on Glen Tanar.

Donald has worked all his life as keeper and gillie. He started on Mar Lodge Estate, where his father was head-keeper. The family lived at Baddoch Lodge and Donald learned his trade from the old keepers, watching them moving with the wind, going out with the ponies, and working with the head-keeper at Balmoral, Mr Gillon.

As a boy, Donald used to go up to Mar in winter to

watch the deer being fed. Everything was 'done' in Gaelic, so Donald was constantly being 'hushed' when he asked what was being said. Often more than 800 deer would be there. The head-keeper always had his rifle nearby, and any old or sick beasts, that wouldn't survive the winter, were shot. The other deer would run away a bit, then come back to the hay.

The heads of the shot beasts were cut off and added to the collection of more than 2,000 which adorned the ballroom at Mar Lodge. A full-time taxidermist worked on the estate, and he was never short of work. The stock of deer was constantly being improved, with additions of stags from Germany and from Windsor.

A special deer drive was held each year, and the King would come over from Balmoral for the day. The drive was always held on a Saturday, much to the annoyance of the gillies and keepers, for this meant they had to spend all Sunday clearing the hill of shot deer.

The head-keeper, another MacDonald, made sure that the shoot was perfectly organised. He knew exactly where the deer were and exactly where to place the men to drive them to the guns.

'I've heard my father say that often twenty or thirty stags would be shot in a day, and I've myself seen as many as seventeen ponies going up the hill to collect them.'

The history of the special deer drives goes back even further. William Scrope, writing in 1838 in *The Art of Deer Stalking*, describes Queen Mary's hunting in 1563: 'The Earl of Atholl prepared for her Majesty's reception by sending out about two thousand Highlanders to gather the deer from Mar, Badenoch, Murray, and Atholl, to the district he had previously appointed. It occupied the Highlanders for several weeks in driving deer, to the amount of two thousand, besides roes, does and other game.

'The Queen, with her numerous attendants and a great concourse of the nobility, gentry, and people, were assembled at the appointed glen, and the spectacle much delighted her Majesty ... The Queen's stag-hounds and those of the nobility were loosed, and a successful chase ensued. Three hundred and sixty deer were killed, five wolves, and some roes.'

In the days of Donald's father, the estate still employed eighteen keepers and gillies. During winter a number of men were employed on forestry work. But the Duke always told the factor to make sure they were not over-worked: 'Now I don't want these men to be slaved on working; just keep them moving and warm because they have to be fit when I come to shoot the stags.'

The laird's word was final, absolute and law. People did what they were told, with no questions asked, or they soon found themselves in trouble. Donald remembers a keeper at Aboyne, John MacKay, losing his job for supposed insolence: 'Lord Dalhousie had arrived, and when John went over in the morning His Lordship asked, "What have you done to the weather, MacKay? Could you not have managed to make a better day of it than this?"

'John replied: "Och, it was fine yesterday. Are you sure you didna bring it with you, My Lord?" Next morning he was called to the factor's office and given his notice.'

Donald MacDonald and Tom MacPhearson have been friends and colleagues all their working lives. Tom lives with his daughter and son-in-law in a small cottage near Ballater and retired from active service a few years ago.

Tom earned his first money when staying on his uncle's farm at the head of Loch Laggan. The estate was owned by Sir John Maxwell Stirling, and the shooting was let to the Rothschilds and the Sasoons. King George V used to shoot there when he was Prince of Wales, and Tom was warned off one evening to mind the gate for the gentlemen.

He remembers seeing the ponies coming down the hill, the Prince of Wales out in front at the gallop. He dashed down to open the gate. That evening, a half-sovereign was sent up from the big house as reward.

During my travels I came across another story of King George V. It was given to me by Robert Howden at Berriedale. A report appeared in a French newspaper on 20 July, 1917, giving a description of the King as a salmon angler. I don't know if the King ever read the article, but it certainly made me smile: *O wad some Power the giftie gie us, to see oursels as ithers see us!*

'THE KING AS A FISHERMAN

'He is an angler of the first force, this King of Britain. Behold him there, as he sits motionless under his umbrella, patiently regarding his many coloured floats. How obstinately he contends with the elements. It is a summer day of Britain. That is to say, it is a day of sleet, and fog and tempest. But what would you? It is as they love it, those who follow the sport.

Presently the King's float begins to descend. The King strikes. My God, how he strikes! The hook is implanted in the very bowels of the salmon. The King rises. He spurns aside his footstool. He strides strongly and swiftly towards the rear. In due time the salmon comes to approach himself to the bank. Aha! The King has cast aside his rod. He hurls himself flat on the ground on his victim. They splash and struggle in the icy water. Name of a dog! But it is a braw laddie! The gillie, a kind of outdoor domestic, administers the *coup de grâce* with a pistol. "The King! Hip-hurrah!". On these red-letter days His Majesty George dines on a haggis and a whisky grog. Like a true Scotsman, he wears only the kilt.'

In Tom's early days, the moor was one of the finest in Scotland. As many as 300 to 400 brace of grouse could be shot in a day. 'Now you are lucky if you see just two', said Tom. 'The birds have just vanished ...'

A keeper's life was always busy, more so recently, since most estates have reduced the numbers of staff on the hill.

Spring was the time for preparing for the coming season: heather-burning, looking for foxes' dens, trapping wild-cats. Tom remembers the biggest wild-cat ever trapped at Invercauld, a beast of forty-nine inches. The laird made a sporran from it.

Then the fishing gentlemen would arrive, and some of the keepers had to act as gillies. The rest would be repairing hill-paths and bridges after the winter floods. Before the end of June all the butts had to be inspected and repaired for the grouse shooting. Then it was stalking and, in November, culling the hinds.

The responsibility for all this work fell on the shoulders of the head-keeper, and he had to be as well organised as any manager in commerce or industry. More so, for he had to contend with the elements as well, and no matter what happened with the weather, everything had to be right when the gentlemen arrived.

Tom's brother also worked as a keeper, on an estate near Loch Maree, in Ross-shire. His house was one-and-a-quarter miles from the lodge, and every morning during the fishing season he had to walk down to be ready to start before nine o'clock. Tom has always been a keen angler and remembers with pleasure great days on Loch Maree.

'In those days, we would go out on the loch and take 20/30 sea-trout regularly, grand fish of up to 14 lb. The best fly was always a Red Spider, tied on a size 10 single hook.'

To the north of Loch Maree, over the vast shoulder of Slioch, is another famous Scottish loch, the Fionn Loch. Its reputation for producing huge brown trout is second to none in Scotland.

Osgood MacKenzie, in his book, *A Hundred Years of Sport in the Highlands*, gives details of the great catches of trout from Fionn.

'How perfectly do I remember one evening in April 1851 (when I was just nine years old), Sir Alexander Gordon Cumming of Altyre sending down a message to us at Pool House, asking my mother and me to come up to the inn and witness the weighing of the fish he had brought back that day, in case his own statements might be doubted in future years.

'There were four beauties lying side by side on the table of the small drinking room, and they turned the scales at 51 lb. The total weight of the twelve fish caught that 12th day of April by trolling was 87 lb 12 oz, made up thus: 14 lb 8 oz, 12 lb 8 oz, 12 lb 4 oz, 12 lb 10 oz, 6 lb 12 oz, 6 lb 8 oz, 3 lb, 3 lb, 2 lb 12 oz, 2 lb 8 oz, 2 lb.'

But perhaps the best record was that made by Mr F. C. McGrady. I give a copy of his own account of his fishing on Fionn Loch.

INVEREWE, POOLEWE, JUNE–JULY, 1912

	Trout	Weight		Trout	Weight
May 30	24	8 lb 8 oz	June 27	71	24 lb 8 oz
May 31	77	28 lb	June 28	83	29 lb 8 oz
June 1	72	31 lb 8 oz	June 29	14	13 lb
June 3	60	21 lb	July 1	68	23 lb
June 4	74	28 lb	July 2	8	3 lb 8 oz
June 5	23	8 lb 8 oz	July 3	95	46 lb
June 6	134	48 lb	July 4	68	25 lb
June 7	180	62 lb	July 5	67	26 lb
June 8	189	74 lb 12 oz	July 6	41	22 lb 8 oz
June 10	187	63 lb 8 oz	July 8	63	23 lb
June 11	119	42 lb	July 9	116	41 lb
June 12	97	35 lb	July 10	76	27 lb
June 13	32	9 lb	July 11	51	19 lb 8 oz
June 14	96	50 lb	July 12	31	25 lb
June 15	160	70 lb	July 13	18	10 lb
June 17	222	74 lb	July 15	71	27 lb
June 18	108	45 lb 8 oz	July 17	20	6 lb 8 oz
June 19	85	31 lb 8 oz	July 18	60	22 lb 8 oz
June 20	154	47 lb 8 oz	July 19	71	24 lb
June 22	55	20 lb	July 20	38	15 lb
June 24	133	46 lb	July 22	25	29 lb 8 oz
June 26	31	22 lb	July 23	40	10 lb 8 oz

July 24	15	6 lb	
July 25	55	23 lb 8 oz	(Total: 3,625 trout, 1,410 lb)
July 26	48	20 lb	

NOTE OF HEAVY TROUT

June 14	1	5 lb 8 oz	July 6	1	3 lb
June 14	1	6 lb	July 12	1	6 lb 12 oz
June 17	1	4 lb	July 12	1	3 lb
June 26	1	7 lb 4 oz	July 15	1	3 lb
June 29	1	3 lb 8 oz	July 22	1	8 lb 4 oz
July 1	2	3 lb each	July 22	1	7 lb
July 3	1	7 lb 8 oz	July 22	1	3 lb 8 oz

All small trout (under 6 inches) were thrown back

Even today the Fionn Loch produces 'monster' trout, but they are not so easy to catch as in Osgood MacKenzie's time, and one can't help wondering what these anglers wanted with all those fish.

Tom MacPhearson certainly enjoyed his days in Ross-shire with his brother, but he had heard so much about the shooting, stalking and fishing on Deeside that he came over to Glen Tanar and worked there for many years before taking his last position on the Invercauld Estate.

The largest salmon he landed on the Dee was a fish of 45 lb, caught when he was gillieing for Arthur Wood. The fish may still be seen in the tackle-shop in Ballater, although when Tom and Arthur Wood caught the salmon, the shop was a saddler's.

Tom always found that his foreign gentlemen were the most unpredictable, both on river and hill. One day he found the laird crouched on the floor of his butt. He asked him what was the matter.

'First that fellow down there got me, and when I was watching him, damn it, but didn't the chap on the other side catch me in the shoulder. It's just not safe, and here I'm staying until it's over!'

The laird's jacket was shredded, as though it had been

put through a mincer. The following day Tom was loading for the laird, watching carefully. He saw the next gun, a gentleman from China, swinging round to his left and just had time to call out a warning to the laird. They both flopped like partridge and avoided serious injury by half-a-second.

'Now, Sir', Tom said to the gentleman. 'That was very nearly your best shot of the day, the laird and his head-keeper with one barrel.' If the gentleman had not been told off much before in his life, he certainly learned a thing or two that day when the laird got to him. He was never seen on the hill again.

During his many years as a keeper, Tom has seen many fine shots. The best he remembers was Ian Walker, of Walker's Whisky. King George V never missed, and Admiral Beattie was also a good hand with the gun.

But some of the best shots he has stalked with have been ladies, although, as Tom said, not everyone can stalk to a lady.

'I remember one old keeper at Invercauld who just hated being out on the hill with a lady, and he'd do anything to avoid going. If he couldn't, then they were never long in coming back, and never with a stag. For the old devil always chose the wettest, wildest, most exposed paths, and would have the poor woman frozen and exhausted within the hour.

'Then he would leave her, on the top of some crag, saying: "Now, Madam, you rest here awhile, for you seem very tired, and I'll go and have a bit spy." He had no intention of doing anything other than finding a dry corner in which to have a snooze and a pipe. When he returned, if the lady hadn't gone off home by herself, then she was generally ready to do so when asked.'

Tom's favourite companion on the hill was a lady of middle years. She and her husband came for many seasons, and he always enjoyed his days out with her. She would crawl, uncomplaining, for hours, and Tom had two royals and a thirteen-pointer with her. She was as good a stalker as he was, and she never missed a shot.

But the last time Tom saw her, she had come north on her own, and that day on the hill she missed every shot: eighteen shots and never a thing. In spite of everything Tom tried, the 'spark' seemed to have gone out of her. When Tom asked what was wrong, she wouldn't answer. At the end of the day, as Tom was saying goodbye, he noticed tears on his lady's face. He said nothing, but that was the last he ever saw of her. 'A better stalker or finer companion on the hill I never had', he told me.

CHAPTER 7

High jinks and history at Tillmouth on Tweed

A few miles from Twizel Bridge, on the River Tweed, is the home of Michael Chapman, head gillie of the Tillmouth Park beats. Michael Chapman is in his mid-thirties and has worked as a gillie since leaving school. He is well informed and keeps up-to-date with all things appertaining to salmon-fishing, and his knowledge is based on reading as much as it is on his years of experience on his beloved river.

I asked Michael when he decided to become a gillie. He told me that, as a boy, he had worked with his uncle, William Johnston, one of the best-known and respected gillies on Tweed. William Johnston was as famous as a poet as he was a gillie, and Michael well remembers his uncle reciting streams of verses, seemingly as endless as the river itself.

Much of William Johnston's work was published in the *Berwick Advertiser*, but one of his poems may still be read in the fishing hut at Border Bridge, Coldstream, where Willie gillied for thirty-five years. It is in the form of a memorial to G. R. K. Muglitson, who fished with Willie for many years and died on 10 December, 1953.

The poem not only sums up Willie's attitude to fishing, but seems to me to speak also for many of his fellow-gillies throughout the land.

> *No more the sound of rippling stream,*
> *Or western zephyers lap your barque;*
> *No more the bait in mid-air gleam,*
> *Or rising fish your eye shall mark.*
>
> *But we who live shall oft retell*
> *Of sporting days in merry mood;*
> *How o'er the fish he cast his spell,*
> *His prawning tactics few withstood.*
>
> *How many varied escapades,*
> *Were his throughout the many years;*
> *In sunshine bright or darker shades,*
> *By slaps in caulds or broken weirs.*
>
> *The river Tweed was in his blood*
> *And of her charms he loved to talk;*
> *He revelled in the spring time flood,*
> *In summer low the fish to stalk.*
>
> *How when upon the slab he laid*
> *His half a dozen springers gay;*
> *His laughter through the rafters played,*
> *Turning dull February into May.*
>
> *You've had your day, you've left your mark*
> *On every stone upon these beats;*
> *In future many a past remark*
> *By you shall live as time retreats.*

The Sporting Gentleman's Gentleman

Time's stream has borne you on her wings
Away from all the pain of earth;
But memory like the bubbling springs,
Shall to our minds bring second birth.

Michael was trained by his uncle, but during his first year he was allowed to do nothing other than sit silently in the boat. He was then allowed to row, and if nobody else was fishing, he and his uncle would have a cast.

I met Michael in the Tillmouth Park Hotel on a cold February evening in 1984. He had just returned from the river with a gentleman and we sat talking over a half-pint. I asked the guest how he had got on during the day. As he turned to reply, I noticed that he seemed to have taken a bad knock on the forehead.

'Have you had an accident?' I asked.

You may imagine my embarrassment when I was told, crossly, that the blood had come from his first salmon, landed a few hours previously!

We drove home to Michael's cottage where Mrs Chapman and young Master Chapman greeted us warmly. Michael has fished all his life, and his chance of the job came when his uncle retired. Fishing, as work, and being a gillie does not detract from Michael's pleasure in the sport. He always enjoys seeing his gentleman catch a salmon. But his own preference is for trout fishing, and he loves nothing better than the challenge of placing a dry fly over a rising fish.

He caught his first salmon while he was fishing for trout on the River Till. He had noticed the fish lying behind a stone in the middle of the stream. Armed only with an 8 ft trout rod, Michael took off the small flies and searched in his box for the largest fly he could find. All the hair was carefully stripped from it and an accommodating worm firmly attached to the bare hook.

The salmon rushed for the bait at the first cast, and after a mighty struggle, lasting more than half-an-hour, Michael landed a 9 lb fish. But one of the gentlemen from the hotel appeared just as the fish was being dispatched. Michael stuffed the salmon down one wader and proudly carried it home.

His return, and the fact that he had poached a salmon, was greeted with dismay, and his mother and father gave him one of the longest lectures he had ever received about stealing other people's property. But when Michael's father telephoned the hotel to explain, the manager thanked him and told him just to keep the fish. Any young lad managing to play and land a fresh-run 9 lb fish on a little trout rod deserved to keep it!

Like Michael Chapman, I have always deplored poaching, whether for trout or salmon, and I grow even less tolerant as I grow older. When I come upon supposed fishermen spinning for trout or using half-a-dozen fixed rods round the shores of a remote loch, my blood boils, and many a day out has been spoiled by furious fights with poachers. Even as a boy aged sixteen, I used to get myself into terrible situations when I remonstrated with poachers along the banks of Tweed, and to this day anyone fishing in an illegal fashion is like a red rag to a bull to me.

I would never begrudge the occasional fish, but today whole van-loads are being taken away, and I weary waiting for a more efficient way of protecting our diminishing stocks of salmon and trout.

The story of Michael's first salmon reminded me of a similar tale of two young lads poaching. The story was told to me by the boys' father, Ron Speirs. The family lived at West Linton, near Edinburgh. Close to the village is Lyne Water, a tributary of Tweed, and one evening the boys decided they would go out after dark to try to get a salmon.

Within an hour they had returned with not one fish, but two, both in the order of 10—12 lb. When their parents remonstrated, the boys claimed they had done nothing other than find them in the bushes and carry them home.

Apparently, stumbling along the river bank, chattering and talking, they had disturbed three men with a net. Thinking the approaching children were the bailiffs, the men had abandoned their net, dropped the fish and fled. Pragmatically, Ron surveyed the two dead salmon and decided it was an ill-wind that didn't blow somebody some good. 'What else could I do but keep them?'

One of the most frustrating aspects of working as a gillie is when an 'ill-wind' blows in an incompetent angler. Michael told me that when the gillie is struggling to keep the boat in position and the gentleman has no idea of how to cast or what to do, then it is depressing, soul-destroying work.

His uncle, Willie Johnston, knew exactly how to handle these situations, and Michael recounted with delight how the old gillie managed.

'If his gentleman wasn't fishing very well, Willie would give instruction and advice, and if that didn't do, he would say: "Do you know how to row? Can you hold the boat? Well, just haud her there for a moment or two and I will have a cast."'

'Invariably, Uncle Willie would hook a fish. Then he'd hand the rod to his gentleman so that he could play the salmon. He knew every inch of the river and always waited until the boat was approaching a good lie before having his cast. But it all looked so easy that his gentleman used to think he had the second sight!'

Another of Willie's methods of getting his gentleman a fish was to give a great shout just before the fish took. He would watch the line all the time and if he saw a fish coming, he would roar: 'That's him!' At the same time, he would pull hard on the oars. The gentleman got such a fright that he would jerk the rod upwards and the salmon would hook itself.

The largest salmon Michael has had to his own rod was a fine fish of 30 lb, but he got little credit for it. His gentleman that day was a Mr Woodcock, a man of advancing years, and after they had worked hard all day, only one fish was on the bank. They were resting from their labours when the big fish rose and Mr Woodcock asked Michael to have a cast at it, since he was too tired. The salmon took after the third cast, and eventually Michael managed to beach him.

The following week a fine photograph appeared in the *Berwick Advertiser* of the salmon being proudly displayed by Mr Woodcock, and to this day a photograph in the hotel shows Mr Woodcock and 'his' 30 lb salmon!

Tweed is famous for the size of its autumn salmon. Stories were being told of monster fish as long ago as 1815. Some of the fish were landed and some were not—and some were both, as was recounted by William Scrope not long after the event described below took place.

'In the year 1815, Robert Kerse hooked a clean salmon of about forty pounds in the Makerstoun water, the largest, he says, he ever encountered: fair work he had with him for some hours; till at last Rob, to use his own expression, was "clean dune out." He landed the fish, however, in the end, and laid him out on the channel; astonished, and rejoicing at his prodigious size, he called out to a man on the opposite bank of the river, who had been watching for some time: "Hey, mon, sic a fish!" He then went for a stone to fell him with; but as soon as his back was turned, the fish began to wamble towards the water, and Kerse turned, and jumped upon it; over they both tumbled, and they, line, hook, and all went into the Tweed. The fish was too much for Rob, having broke the line, which got twisted round his leg, and made its escape, to his great disappointment and loss, for at the price clean salmon were then selling, he could have got five pounds for it.'

A few that did not get away were caught more recently. Mr G. McCulloch, fishing at Lower Floors on 20

November, 1903, took 19 salmon weighing 389 lb 8 oz, an average of 20 lb 8 oz per fish. In 1981, Michael was fishing in November with a very good angler, a Mr Dixon, on Beat 6. The third cast of the morning brought a 24 lb fish, and immediately afterwards Mr Dixon hooked a salmon of 24 lb 8 oz. In a never-to-be-forgotten day, they landed six beautiful salmon weighing a total of 128 lb, an average of 21 lb 3 oz.

Tweed's history redounds with similar stories of great catches and great characters, such as Scrope, friend of Walter Scott, and Thomas Tod Stoddart, who lived at Kelso. Stoddart, although trained as a lawyer, never practised anything other than the art of fishing. When asked by the local magistrate what he was doing with himself these days, Stoddart replied unhesitatingly: 'Doing man? I'm an angler!'

Tweed still has more than a fair share of characters, and Michael remembers one of his gentlemen with particular affection: Air-Commodore Hoskins, a friend of Winston Churchill, skilled angler and delightful companion. In spite of being blind, Air-Commodore Hoskins could place a fly with unerring accuracy upon the briefest of directions. He had his own tackle-box and would attend to all his own needs without assistance. In the hotel at night he would remark: 'Saw more than we caught!'

The only time Michael has feared for the life of a guest happened on a windy day when he was out with the Air-Commodore. It was against his better judgement that Michael had launched the boat, but since it was his gentleman's last day, he felt obliged to do so.

A tremendous easterly gale was blowing, and although Michael managed to row up to the top of the beat, he could not get back down. The boat turned sideways on to the current and then struck bottom and began to fill with water. All this time the Air-Commodore sat gripping the sides of the boat, saying nothing. More through good fortune and steady nerves than through skill, Michael brought the situation under control and got his gentleman safely ashore. The only comment the Air-Commodore made was to ask, 'Is this boat leaking, Michael?'

'Leaking?' thought Michael. 'We've both nearly drowned!'

But the Air-Commodore never asked what was happening or interfered, although he must have guessed that something was seriously wrong.

Not all the retired officers for whom Michael has gillied over the years have been such agreeable or trusting companions. The worst row Michael has ever had was with an ex-Indian Army colonel.

The Colonel was about six feet tall and, whether catching fish or not, as bad-tempered as could be. He was a rude old man with whom none of the other gillies would work, which is why he always ended up with Michael.

This particular day was a cold March morning with the wind blowing hard upriver. Snow was whisking by as Michael stood watching the Colonel casting everywhere but to the fish. The bottom, the trees, himself and Michael were all hooked, and the Colonel was a danger to anything within range—other than salmon.

So Michael put him in the boat and remained on the bank, holding a rope attached to the bow. Out there the Colonel had more chance of hooking a fish and far less chance of hooking Michael.

After a particularly violent back-cast, Michael heard the tell-tale crack as the fly departed from the line.

'Colonel! I think the fly has gone', Michael shouted across the wind.

'No it hasn't. I can see it landing', replied the Colonel.

'Are you sure, Colonel?' Michael asked.

'Damn it man! I know what I'm doing! I tell you I can see the fly! Work the boat and be quiet!'

Manoeuvring a boat down a pool on a rope from the bank is no easy task, least of all in a force-six gale during a March spate. Michael was annoyed.

'I think you'd better check just to make sure, Colonel!'

'Will you mind your own business! I tell you I can see the fly and it's fine.'

'Colonel, there is something wrong. You *have* cracked off the fly!'

But the Colonel paid not the slightest attention. The boat was fished slowly and carefully down the length of the pool—and it was a long pool. By the time they had reached the end, Michael was frozen and furious.

'The silly old devil had fished all the way without a fly, and me on the bank like an idiot helping him!'

Michael pulled the boat ashore and the Colonel left the rod in the stern. Without so much as a 'Thank you', he stamped off up the river, calling over his shoulder.

'We'll fish it down again.'

As he marched up the bank, the Colonel took his big hip-flask from his pocket and had a few hefty swigs.

Michael took a fly from his box and quickly attached it to the bare nylon. Then, to collect the line properly, he flicked the fly into the stream.

'Damn me if a 15 lb salmon didn't throw itself out of the water, grab the fly and make off upstream like a rocket!'

As the fish passed the Colonel, the old man turned and saw what was happening. Spluttering into the last mouthful of his dram, he roared at Michael: 'What do you think you're doing? Who gave you permission to fish? Put down that rod immediately!'

The Colonel came rushing down the bank and tried to grab the rod from Michael's hands.

But Michael kept a firm grip and held the enraged Colonel off until he had played and landed the fish. The gentleman was jumping about on the bank, roaring and fuming as Michael killed the fish and handed it to him.

'Now listen, Colonel! I've just about had enough of you and your bad manners. You've wasted a whole morning fishing down the pool without a fly on your cast, in spite of the fact that if I told you once I told you a dozen times to check ...'

'How dare you speak to me like that!' yelled the Colonel.

'... and you were too pig-headed even to pull it in and make sure', continued Michael.

'Nobody talks to me like that!'

Undaunted, Michael continued with unabated anger: 'And this is not the bloody Army, nor am I one of your native bearers!'

'I'll have you sacked the instant I get back to the hotel!'

'Colonel, if you don't mend your manners, you may never get back to the hotel. I'm very tempted to chuck you straight into the river—now!'

Michael took a couple of threatening steps towards the Colonel, who backed away apprehensively.

'D'you understand me, Colonel? I'm not spending the whole afternoon hauling you about the river in a blizzard and you without even a fly on the end of your cast. Make up your mind: do as you are told or get the hell out of it! Which is it to be?'

The Colonel was visibly shaken. He quietened down and, eventually, apologised for his bad temper. He even offered Michael a dram from his flask, and for the rest of the afternoon he behaved perfectly. The morning's 'incident' was never mentioned and three good salmon were caught. Having a fly on the end of the line helped the Colonel enormously, and from that moment onwards, a nicer man could not be found anywhere on the river.

'There comes a time', said Michael, 'when you have to put a stop to such nonsense, or there'd be no end to it.'

As in so many other aspects of salmon-fishing, Michael's experience with his uncle had stood him in good stead. Old Willie Johnston was a patient man—up to a point. But beyond that point he would not go. He had a retired Admiral out one morning and was being given directions about what to do and where to go as fast as Tweed in spate.

Eventually, Willie turned to the Admiral and said: 'Now, Admiral, when you're on the bridge of your ship, it is you who'll give the orders. But when you're in my ship, I give the commands. If that isn't to your liking, we can go ashore any time you choose.'

Willie had no more trouble and was able to get on with the job in hand in peace and quiet: putting his gentleman over the fish.

Most of the gillies to whom I have talked have had but a poor opinion of spinning and bait-fishing for salmon, and have considered modern flies—Waddingtons, tube-flies and the likes—to be little better: 'When they have to resort to raking about the bottom with lumps of iron to catch salmon, then I want nothing to do with it!'

I subscribe to their view with regards to spinning, but the argument concerning the use of tube-flies is harder to follow. Like everything else in life, fashions change. What we consider to be 'traditional' salmon flies now—Green Highlander, Jock Scott, Silver Wilkinson, Hairy Mary— were greeted with that same suspicion when they were first introduced.

'The fashion in flies has changed on the Tweed, as on most other Scottish waters. The gaudiest colours, the brightest tinsel, the most daring combinations are displayed in the lures now in vogue ...' Thus an editorial comment in William Scrope's book, *Days and Nights Salmon Fishing in the Tweed*, published in the early years of the nineteenth century.

The tried and trusted patterns of these years were much less gaudy specimens. The six flies most favoured by Scrope—Kinmont Willie, The Lady of Mertoun, Toppy, Michael Scott, Meg With the Muckle Mouth, and Meg in Her Braws, were dressed for him by his gillie, Charles Purdie. Although some of the materials used may be difficult or impossible to come by today, it it tempting to try these old patterns again. They worked well enough in days gone by, why not now?

KINMONT WILLIE

Wings:	Mottled feather from under the wing of a male teal.
Head:	Yellow wool.
Body:	Fur of the hare's ear.
End of body:	Red wool.
Tail:	Yellow wool.
Round the body:	Black cock's hackle.

THE LADY OF MERTOUN

Wings:	Mottled feather from under the wings of the male teal.
Head:	Crimson wool.
Body:	Water-rat's fur.
End of body:	Crimson wool.
Tail:	Yellow wool.
Round the body:	Black cock's hackle.
End of body:	A little red hackle.

TOPPY

Wings:	Black feather from a turkey's tail, tipped with white.
Head:	Crimson wool.
Body:	Black bullock's hair.
End of body:	Crimson wool.
Tail:	Yellow wool.
Body:	Black cock's hackle.
End of body:	Small piece of red cock's hackle.

MICHAEL SCOTT ('A most killing wizard')

Wings:	Mottled feather from the back of a drake.
Head:	Yellow wool, with a little hare's fur next to it.
Body:	Black wool.
End of body:	Fur from the hare's ear; next to the hare's ear, crimson wool.
Tail:	Yellow wool.
Round the body:	Black cock's hackle.
End of body:	Red cock's hackle.
Round the body:	Gold twist, spirally.

MEG WITH THE MUCKLE MOUTH

Wings:	From the tail of a brown turkey.
Head:	Crimson wool.
Body:	Yellow silk.
End of body:	Crimson wool.
Tail:	Yellow or orange wool.
Round the tail:	Red cock's hackle.
Round the body:	Gold twist; over it, hackle mixed with colour as above.

MEG IN HER BRAWS

Wings:	Light brown, from the wing of a bittern.
Head:	Yellow wool.
Next the head:	Mottled blue feather from a jay's wing.
Body:	Brown wool mixed with bullock's hair.
End of body:	Green wool; next to the crimson wool.
Tail:	Yellow wool.
Round the body:	Gold twist; over that, cock's hackle, black at the roots and red at the points.

The noise of the telephone broke into our conversation and thoughts, and while Michael answered it, advising a gentleman due to arrive in a few days, I busied myself with my hip-flask and two glasses. Thinking of Michael's near-disaster with Air-Commodore Hoskins, I asked him if gentlemen tended to get themselves into difficulties often. Michael smiled.

'Now there are some gentlemen who will just never do what they're told. I had a veterinary surgeon out with me once and every time he hooked a fish he insisted on being put ashore to play it.

'Now, that's not really necessary unless it's a very big fish. Even then, most can be landed from the boat. Rowing backwards and forwards from the shore only wastes good fishing time. My gentleman would go dancing about the bank as though he were playing a whale.

'He was going through this performance with a fish of about 8 lb when I saw the danger and called to him to watch out for a deep hole to his right. Hardly were the words out of my mouth than in he went! When he surfaced,

I managed to grab him, and he still had the rod firmly grasped!

'Well, we landed the salmon and he decided to return to the hotel to change his clothes. Now his wife was with him, and she had never fished before, so I suggested that, rather than sit waiting, we had a few casts, because the river was full of fish.

'You'd be surprised at the number of gentlemen I meet who have pretty young wives, and this lady was no exception. This was in the days when the mini-skirt was popular, and I can see the lady yet, sat on the fishing stool, her skirt half-way up to her waist.

'But she was game to learn and soon had the hang of getting the fly out. We fished away for about twenty minutes until I saw her husband's car approaching the fishing hut. At that moment a fish grabbed the fly and tore line from the reel in a mighty run.

'The young lady got such a fright that she screamed in terror, toppled backwards and knocked me clean off the thwart into the bow. There we both were, in a tangled heap, her legs in the air, the skirt anywhere, shouting and bawling as the salmon went daft astern. I was trying to get my hands round her waist to grab the rod and she was pushing and shoving, trying to sit upright.

'Her husband took one look at the situation and screeched to a halt, leapt from the car and came running down the bank, shaking his fist and shouting at me to stop whatever I was doing. "Hold on, dear!" he shouted. "I'm coming!" With which he dashed in and within moments found himself floundering about up to his neck once more.

'Somehow I managed to get him ashore and told him not to be stupid: "Grab the rod and mind the salmon, and I'll take care of the lady." He went red as a beetroot when he realised what had happened, but he landed the fish with good grace.

' "Damn it!" he said. "I'm soaked to the skin again!"

'I suggested that he went back to the hotel to change

once more, but that this time he took his lady with him. It was either that or I could see myself spending the whole day hauling him, and not salmon, from the river. But he came back alone. I suspect his lady had had enough salmon-fishing to last her the rest of her life!'

More and more present-day gentlemen are visitors from overseas, and sometimes the language barrier presents insurmountable problems. Michael had two Belgian gentlemen recently, neither of whom understood much English, while Michael certainly had little of their language. Everything had to be done by signs and gesticulation. It was a bitterly cold morning towards the end of February, and every so often Michael had to clear ice from the rings of their rods. But, like most foreign gentlemen, they were as keen as mustard, lashing away as though their very lives depended on catching a salmon.

Fish were showing all over the deep pool throughout the morning, but none was in taking mood. Then, suddenly the pool went quiet. The reason soon became clear: a seal had entered the pool and was staring curiously at the boat from a distance of about ten yards.

Michael tried to tell his gentlemen, but the English word 'seal' must have sounded very like the French word for 'sky'. For instead of looking to where Michael was pointing, the two anglers stared heavenwards, wondering what their strange gillie was yammering on about. The more Michael shouted, 'Seal!', the harder they stared at the sky.

As luck would have it, a salmon of about 20 lb chose that moment to grab one of the lures. The Belgian gentleman whose rod it was got such a shock that he almost fell out of the boat in surprise; but in spite of all Michael could do to divert his attention, he continued searching the sky for the supposed danger, and never saw the fish until it was in the bottom of the boat!

The seal had long since disappeared, so Michael gave up trying to explain. The gentlemen obviously thought him soft in the head, anyway, and a dangerous character to be watched carefully.

The day was so cold that the gentlemen indicated they wanted to be put ashore. Once there, they began collecting up the driftwood and rubbish that littered the banks to make a fire. As they did so, Michael noticed a number of empty aerosol cans among the heap and tried to warn them of the danger before they lit their fire.

The gentlemen paid no attention and soon had a mighty blaze raging. Michael retired to a safe distance to await events. The first can exploded with a sound like a rifle-shot, quickly followed by two more. The gentlemen looked round at Michael, leapt to their feet and, abandoning rods, tackle and dignity, took to their heels, convinced that Michael had finally taken leave of his senses and was intent on murdering them both.

It took Michael a mile to catch them and half-an-hour to calm them down. But some good came of it, because by the time they were finished, they were as warm as could be, although they watched their gillie like hawks for the rest of their stay.

One of Michael's gentlemen presented a different problem to gillies. He was unable to walk very well and required constant assistance while walking down to the river and getting in and out of the boat. Most gillies are delighted to offer all the help their gentlemen need, but old Mr Meredith could never be pleased and used to lead his gillies a merry dance.

Other guests came in for their fair share of Mr Meredith's hectoring habits, too. No matter what was done, he had done it before, better, more skilfully, and more often. Michael had him out one day on Beat 4 when a lot of kelts were at the end of the beat. After fishing the top water, Michael suggested they should have a cast down below, but Mr Meredith would have none of it, claiming that the lower water held only kelts and not a fresh fish among them.

Michael explained that it is often possible to separate kelts from clean fish, and that it is always worth at least the attempt. The following day his guest was a lady angler who had been told by Mr Meredith that she was wasting her time on Beat 4, since it held only kelts.

Michael mounted a Toby and they fished the beat down, taking three kelts within the hour. He then mounted a sprat and had his lady fish it deep and slow. The result was that they took four beautiful fresh-run salmon, the sea-lice still on them. That evening in the hotel, the tables were turned. For once Mr Meredith had no answer when asked how it had been done.

The following day, after being helped into the boat, Mr Meredith announced that he had to be in for lunch at 12.30 prompt, since he was entertaining a friend. David, who was head gillie at the time, asked Michael if he would help get Mr Meredith up to the fishing hut, but as soon as the boat reached the shore they were amazed to see Mr Meredith leap from the boat and go dancing off unaided to the hut.

Shortly afterwards a huge Bentley drew up and an attractive young lady got out and joined Mr Meredith in the hut. The river rang with the sounds of their laughter. The gillies had never seen their gentleman smile, let alone laugh. After an hour or so, the door opened and the lady took her leave, blowing Mr Meredith a farewell kiss as she went. 'Tight lines!' she called.

As the car disappeared, Mr Meredith shouted over to the gillies and demanded that they get a move on and help him down to the boat. David, the head gillie, went over to the gentleman. Standing inches from the agitated face of the expectant angler, David said: 'Now listen you here! You may stand there for as long as you bloody well like; but if you can run up to the fishing hut before lunch, you can walk back down after it, and you'll find me waiting ready whenever you are!' With which David turned his back and marched off to the boat.

Michael told me there has always been a great deal of friendly rivalry between the gillies on the south and north banks of Tweed, and for years David had a running battle with his 'arch-enemy', Frank Binnie, at Tweed Mill on 'the other side'. They watched each other constantly, and many a slanging match was held across the river.

'Have you no one with you today, Binnie?'

'Oh, aye! He's coming in an hour or so.'

'Get yourself in then, man, and make your Woodbine money before he arrives!'

One morning, walking to the river, David stopped and said to Michael: 'Look! There's Binnie. What's he up to? What's he doing?'

Michael handed David the binoculars and told him to look for himself. Frank Binnie seemed to be hiding behind a bush, looking towards them.

'What's he doing? I can't see. What's he doing?' asked David.

Grabbing the glasses, Michael focused on Frank. The old man was crouched behind the bush, his own binoculars pressed to his eyes, staring across at them. Turning to his companion, Michael exclaimed: 'Doing? He's as daft as you are. He's spying on you just as you're spying on him! It's damned few fish either of you will catch until you stop this nonsense!'

It was late evening before I thanked Michael and made my farewells. Frost sparkled on the road and as I drove home a well-known saying came to mind: 'What is a gentleman without his recreations?' It seemed to me that the answer was: 'Not very much'—and even less without the services of a good gillie. Michael Chapman is one of the best.

CHAPTER 8

Three Sutherlands, Helmsdale and Caithness

Suddenly, it's spring. The long Caithness winter has ended. Sunlight sparkles on Loch Watten. Snowy buds speck willows, and lapwings swoop and somersault over bright green fields. A flock of wild swans peck and preen in new grass, fidgeting, anxious to be gone. At noon they straggle skywards, heading towards their distant Arctic breeding grounds.

Southwards from my window, across fields busy with lambing, the Caithness mountains line the horizon: Scaraben, Morven, Smean, Ben Alisky and Beinn Glaschoire. Westwards, in Sutherland, over desolate moorlands, Ben Hope and Ben Loyal pierce billowy white clouds. Eastwards, overlooking the wide blue sweep of Sinclair Bay, stands the 'exclamation mark' of Stevenson's lighthouse on the cliffs of Noss Head. All around, spring sparkles, as though the year has opened its doors and invited summer in.

Caithness is a county of contrasts: towering, sea-bird-clad crags; dramatic, cliff-top castles; deserted shining white beaches; Iron Age burial chambers and Pictish forts; tiny harbours, crouched between jagged stacks; the ominous bulk of Dounreay Atomic Power Station.

The Royal Burgh of Wick, clustered around shallow, skerrie-strewn Wick Bay, is the county town. The main industry used to be fishing, and Wick Harbour still boasts a sizeable fleet. But in days gone by, it was the foremost herring fishing station in Europe. In 1835 alone, 106 million herring were landed, and more than 1,100 small vessels crowded the water-front. Thousands of Highlanders flocked to the town during the fishing season: women and girls to work as gutters and packers; men to hire-on as crew in tiny sailing boats.

My grandfather was born near Wick, in the small fishing village of Staxigoe. All along the Caithness coast are other, similar harbours, once bustling with activity, now havens for lobster and crab fishermen.

One of the most dramatic of these harbours lies a few miles south of Wick, at Whalligoe, where 365 steps, cut into the face of an almost sheer cliff, lead down to a jetty and mooring-place. In days gone by, women-folk toiled up these steps carrying heavy baskets of herring on their heads. But Whalligoe Steps are as well cared for today as they were when busy with tired fisher-folk. A local lady weeds them regularly. Her belief is that since the Good Lord was a fisherman himself, when he comes again, he may choose to land at Whalligoe. So the steps must be kept tidy and ready.

The 'land of John o'Groats' is bounded on the west and south by Sutherland. Here, straths and glens are scattered with the ruins of crofters' homes—the homes of people evicted to make way for sheep during the terrible times of the Highland Clearances:

'At daybreak, on a cold April morning in 1819, Mr Patrick Sellar, accompanied by the fiscal, a strong body of constables, sheriff officers and others, arrived at the small village of Grummore on the north shore of Loch Naver. The inhabitants of the sixteen dwellings were ordered to remove themselves and their belongings from their homes, and half-an-hour later the cottages were set on fire and destroyed.'

Thus began the infamous Strathnaver Clearances, when 2,000 men, women and children were made homeless.

Mr Patrick Sellar and his colleagues did their evil work well, for the descendants of the folk who tended the black cattle and crops of the far north are now scattered throughout the world.

Properly to appreciate the vastness of this remote land, you should climb to the top of Scotland's most northern 'munro', Ben Hope. Look eastwards over jagged Ben Loyal to Strathnaver and Ben Klibreck; northwards, across the Kyle of Tongue's golden sands to Orkney and Ward Hill on Hoy; west and south to grey Foinaven, Arkle and Ben Stack, near Scourie; to mighty Ben More Assynt, Suilven, Canisp, Cul Mor and Cul Beag in the Inverpolly National Nature Reserve; and, out in the Atlantic, on the misty horizon, to a distant prospect of Lewis, the 'heather isle' of the Outer Hebrides.

These are the last great wilderness lands of Scotland, where you may walk all day without meeting another soul, or share the lonely solitude of a remote lochan with otter or red-throated diver. Here are raven and red deer, and secret corries where a sudden storm can swoop down, leaving even the best-prepared traveller cold and gasping; where the shimmering heat of a blistering summer day can lull you to drowsy sleep on a tree-fringed sandy shore.

Above all, Caithness and Sutherland have some of the finest game-fishing and stalking in the world. For decades, sportsmen have trekked north in search of adventure and to fish the matchless rivers, Helmsdale, Thurso, Naver and Dionard, for salmon; the glorious lochs, Hope, Stack and More, for silvery sea-trout; the hundreds of lochs and lochans in the moors and mountains around Scourie, Altnaharra, Melvich, Altnabreac and Forsinard for wild brown trout; the crystal-clear limestone waters of Durness for shy, monster brown trout; and Loch St John's and Loch Watten on the Caithness plain for their perfectly shaped trout.

I was introduced to Scotland's far north and its never-ending delights by considerate parents. Appreciating, but not really fully understanding, my love of fishing, they determined upon a holiday in Strathnaver. It was as though I had been given a glimpse of heaven, and I knew that, sooner or later, I would come to live among the lonely moorlands and empty hills.

We stayed with a lady named—not surprisingly—MacKay, mid-way down the strath. Mrs MacKay was of the old school: hell-fire and brimstone on Sunday, and off at one minute past midnight to net the river on Monday. I fished the estuary of the Naver for salmon and spent long, unforgettable hours walking the hills and narrow burns in search of brown trout.

Many years later I did return, with my wife, Ann, and our own children. We came to live in Caithness and we made the pilgrimage to Scourie. We have been going back ever since.

Last year we climbed to a small loch near Foinaven. I cast over the reeds along the rocky shore and as my flies landed, the surface exploded. Two ¾ lb trout each grabbed a fly simultaneously. They were lean and hungry, deeply marked, tinged with green. Our day ended with a basket of 11 fish kept, weighing 9 lb, and with wet feet, tired legs and wind-burned faces. The hardest part was leaving. Evening sunlight shadowed the grey mountains and golden plover piped as we made our way down the track by mirror-calm lochs stippled with the rings of rising trout. A black-throated diver swept by, neck outstretched, calling hauntingly ... It was all that is best in fishing, all that fishing means to me.

Most of the fish I caught that day were taken on a fly called the Willie Ross. This pattern combines all the virtues of the Black Pennell, Soldier Palmer and Butcher: black, silver and red. Willie Ross, who devised the fly, was one of the Altnaharra gillies, an expert fisherman endowed with endless patience, and friend and mentor to many an anxious angler.

Willie died some years ago, but an excellent impression of the man, and the Altnaharra fishings, has been left by Stephen Johnson in his book, *Fishing from Afar*. Stephen Johnson was shot down in December, 1942, over Germany, and incarcerated in Stalag Luft III. He wrote his book during his imprisonment and tells of his time with Willie Ross ...

'The river Mudale runs into Loch Naver by the hotel, and Willie Ross, the gillie, had caught a fish out of it a fortnight before we arrived, so we thought it was probably quite a good chance.

'We usually fished it in the evening, after a day on the loch and a good tea to warm us up again, as the best pools were quite near the hotel, but I spent one whole day on it.

'Willie and I started after breakfast with our lunch in our pockets and we fished the whole river (which is about six miles long) from the bottom to the top and back again. Willie took his "wand", which was a 12 ft greenheart, and I had a big, strong 10 ft sea-trout rod.

'The river runs through fairly boggy country and there was no shelter from the bitterly cold wind and frequent snow showers. The country was looking as bleak and desolate as only Sutherland can in a cold, late spring. The distant hills were covered with snow and the sky was a dark grey with occasional breaks of greenish-blue and gleams of watery sunshine. The heather and grass were still the brown of winter, with an occasional sheep showing white against it.

'We fished alternate pools, Willie leaving me the best places, with instructions as to where to fish, and going on to the next pool himself. He set a great pace. Part of the time I froze when I was fishing, while the rest I was sweating to try and catch him up.

'We had lunch sheltering behind a low stone wall as a particularly bad snowstorm blew over, leaving the moor with a sprinkling of white on grass and heather. After lunch we fished on up as far as some falls and then turned for home, fishing only the best places on the way back; but as we passed pools Willie told me of fish that had been hooked, lost and landed in them, probably for the last twenty years ...

'I asked him about the largest fish he had ever seen. It was a sad tale. A gentleman had hooked a monstrous salmon in a pool on the Naver. Willie couldn't even make a guess at its weight, although he had seen it clearly several times.

'The gentleman played the fish for many hours, but he had a wife and she wore the pants, for when it was time to go home for tea she said so in no uncertain voice, "and the gentleman cut the line and left the fish".

'There was no doubt by the tone in which Willie said it as to which of the two, wife or fish, he should have left. I am sure that Willie thinks that a man can marry a wife any day, but perhaps only one day in a lifetime is there a chance of landing a record salmon. He is the keenest fisherman I have ever met, and although we had a blank day on the Mudale, it was a pleasure spending it with him.

'We were kindly given a few days on the River Naver ... and the second day Willie Ross insisted on coming with me. As he knew the water well, he was quite invaluable. There is a road down the valley, and when there is plenty of petrol in the land it is easier to use a car to go from pool to pool, but we had none, so we walked. If we wanted to fish the whole beat thoroughly, there was no time to be lost between pools, and Willie was always away to the next pool at a terrific pace before I could get my line wound in from the last cast in the previous pool.

'As I was wearing waders and he wasn't, I became very hot trying to keep up with him. I have never seen any other gillie half as keen on catching salmon.

'We had seen a few fresh fish move in one pool on our way down, so we made for it fairly quickly with just a few casts into the most likely spots in the other pools as we passed. This particular pool was at a bend in the river, with the stream coming across to our bank and running strongly down it for the last half of the pool ...

'At the very end of the pool the line tightened ... and I was into a fish. There was no doubt he was fresh as he jumped almost at once and showed himself a thick, clean fish of about 15 lb.

'He kept well out in the middle of the river and went downstream among white broken water and stones. I had to run down to get opposite him and then hold my rod as high as possible to prevent the line between myself and the fish getting round a stone—"drowned and cut" as Scrope describes it.

'He began tiring after a time and came to our side of the pool, but there was no easy place from which to gaff him, as there were big stones in a few feet of water right up to the bank.

'Willie, without a moment's hesitation, was in the freezing water up to the knees, wading out to a clear spot beyond the stones. The fish made one more rush into the fast water while Willie crouched, as still as a heron, and waited for him to be brought within reach. He came slowly into slacker water, fighting every inch of the way. Willie gaffed him and started wading ashore. The fly fell out of his mouth just as Willie stepped on to the bank with water dripping from his breeches, but we had him, a lovely fish of 17 lb and covered with sea-lice.'

Although I never had the pleasure of meeting Willie Ross, I did meet Mrs Ross and Willie's daughter, Mrs Jean Sharp, who is Postmistress at Altnaharra. Alan Finch, of the Altnaharra Hotel, took me across one cold winter night and we sat in front of a blazing fire, talking of the old days, when up to fifteen gillies worked from the hotel.

Mrs Ross told me that Willie was 'fishing mad: just as happy getting nothing as he was getting a big catch'. But Willie held the record among the gillies for the largest catch from Loch Naver, and there is a fine photograph of the fish in Jean Sharp's lounge: 'June 10, nine salmon weighing 119 lb taken on the fly by Gilbert Lawrence Saurin with Willie Ross as gillie'. The photograph is inscribed: 'In happy memory of a sackful'.

Willie worked all his life at Altnaharra. When he started, his wages were thirty-two shillings a week, for the fishing season only. In winter he had to take odd jobs and trap rabbits to make ends meet. He was given no suit of clothes, either, as were the keepers, but there was the occasional good tip of fifteen shillings, although the standard rate was more in the order of five shillings. But, as Mrs Ross explained, 'Willie never complained. After all, you don't argue with your breakfast and dinner, do you?'

Over the years the great and famous have come to Altnaharra to fish Naver and Hope, and Willie gillied and worked for many of them. John Player used to come and give Willie hell for smoking Capstan. The publishing family, Outram, were regular visitors. The Queen Mother, Prince Charles, the Duke of Beaufort and Lord Moncrief all came. Yet few will be as well remembered or as often blessed as the man who invented that incomparable fly, Willie Ross.

The idea of being a gillie is a romantic one much beloved of those who work in town and city. They dream of 'packing it all in', getting away to the Highlands, and earning a few pounds here and there as a gillie—just enough to live.

Fortunately, it remains a dream for most, because the reality of living and working in the far north is a far cry from their imagined rustic idyll. And, believe me, being a gillie is not all fun and laughter.

Each year, for one reason or another, I find myself in a boat with a visitor to the north. Often, an angler has written asking for advice or information, but on meeting him I quickly realise that he has no idea of how to tackle a Scottish trout loch. Rather than see him waste precious holiday-time, I am often tempted into offering to gillie for a day, to start him off on the right foot, so to speak.

Ann and I recently went over to meet a couple of visiting anglers who were staying at the Ulbster Arms Hotel in Halkirk. I asked about the casts and flies they intended to use. The gentleman explained that they used casts 6 ft long, with two flies attached to 18-inch droppers. So I offered to take them out the following day on Loch Watten. This gave me the opportunity of showing them how to make up a traditional Scottish loch cast: 10/12 ft, with three flies on 3-inch droppers.

Surprisingly few of the folk I meet can really cast. Sure, they can roll out a long line with the aid of a carbon-fibre rod, but they are no more capable of delicately putting a fly over the nose of a rising trout than they are of flying.

Most men use far too much strength when casting. The result is that cast and line land in a huge heap around their ears—a 'fankle' or 'bugger's muddle'. If they pass you the rod, then more often than not a few shakes will put matters to rights; but they sit there, with their pride and their fankle, picking away, muttering and cursing: 'New rod, you know. Not quite the action I expected'; or, 'That's the trouble with fishing light in a wind.' The cast is probably 6 lb b/s!

Alan Finch, who owns the Altnaharra Hotel, often has to stand in as a gillie. He told me that he once had two beginners out on Loch Naver. It wasn't windy, but even so, the bow rod managed to get his fly stuck in Alan's left ear at exactly the same moment that the stern rod caught him in the right.

As he sat there, draped and furious, the bow said to the stern: 'What do you think we should do with him, Andrew?'

'Throw him back', replied Andrew. 'He's foul-hooked!'

They offered Alan a dram to 'take away the pain', to which he replied: 'Certainly, but if either of you two gentlemen does that again, it's the pair of you that I'll be taking away, straight back to the fishing-hut.'

That is why many gillies wear deer-stalker hats with the flaps tied well down: to protect their ears—apart, that is, from Angus MacKay. Angus has never put the flaps of his deer-stalker down since 'the accident'.

It happened one cold March day on Loch Oich in Inverness-shire. Visibility was down to a few yards and Angus could barely see his gentleman through the snow. But he could hear the *swish, swish*, of the salmon-fly close by his head, so had his flaps down, just in case. But when the gentleman offered Angus a good dram to ward off the cold, he never heard a word. From that day to this, Angus has never again tied down the flaps of his hat!

Whisky, and the love of it, has become part of the mythology of being a gillie. While I would not deny that many gentlemen's gentlemen enjoy a good dram, they do so no more than their masters, and in many cases, a lot less.

But there is no doubt in my mind that whisky, taken in moderation and with due care and respect, can make the difference between catching fish or not. Two years ago I was out in the hills with three friends: Roy Eaton, then editor of *Trout and Salmon*, the late Bill Smelt, and a farmer friend of mine, Sandy Bremner.

At the start of the day I offered my flask round, and everyone, except Bill, had what we call 'a small sensation'. Bill refused, saying that it was a bit early in the day. By lunch-time we had all caught fish—except Bill. After lunch I again offered my flask, and again Bill refused. I explained that having a dram was more a gesture than a drink, and that it helped you to relax and cast more easily. Bill still refused. At the end of the day everyone had caught trout—except Bill.

The same happened the following day when we walked out to fish Loch Garbh, which is full to overflowing with hard-fighting, hungry trout. By lunch-time we had all caught fish—except Bill.

'What am I to do?' he exclaimed.

'Have a dram, Bill, have a dram.'

He did, and on the first cast after lunch he hooked his first Caithness wild brown trout.

I explained to Bill that that was the reason gentlemen always took along a dram for their gillies. But Bill was still sceptical.

'What would happen if I went out with no whisky?'

I remembered asking the same question of an old gillie in Ayrshire, and I gave Bill the reply I had received.

'Well, then, Bill, as likely as not the gillie would just take you to where there were no fish!'

The southern border between Caithness and Sutherland, where the road follows sheer cliffs, twisting and winding northwards from Helmsdale, is known as the Ord of Caithness. It is a dangerous place in winter, when snow drifts over the road. A few years ago several folk perished, trapped in their cars in a blizzard.

It was even more dangerous in the past. In the Middle Ages the Ord was guarded by a Caithness robber-baron named Grey Steel. His main objective in life, apart from terrorising half the north, was to way-lay travellers on the Ord and demand payment for passage over it.

If Grey Steel was not satisfied with the amount offered, the wretched traveller was thrown over the cliffs to his death. Grey Steel lived on a small island in Loch Rangag, and the remains of his castle may still be seen today as you drive north from Latheron towards Thurso.

Throughout history, while the southern Scots pursued their normal activities—blackmail, murder, plotting, clan warfare, strife and rebellion—the people of the far north carried on their own personal feuds:

> *Sinclair, Sutherland, Keith and Clan Gunn,*
> *There never was peace where these four were in*

They were, and are, a hard-headed, independent people, slow to anger and quick to strike back.

When King Haakon of Norway was on his way to defeat and disaster at the Battle of Largs in 1261, his great fleet rested in Loch Eribol on the north coast of Sutherland, but briefly. The foraging party sent ashore was quickly massacred by the Clan MacKay. Since the Norwegians had no time to go chasing round the wilds of the Forest of Reay, the deaths of their comrades were left unavenged.

In the Middle Ages, the Lord of the Forest of Reay had a hunting lodge near the site of the present house at the western end of Loch Stack. It was customary, on his arrival, for tenants to send gifts to the lodge.

One of the tenants, who lived on an island in a loch nearby, sent his wife down with a gift of two fine hares. But Lord Reay fancied the wife more than the hares, and asked her to stay with him. The lady replied: 'Not while my husband is alive.' Whereupon, Lord Reay despatched two of his henchmen into the hills to seek out the husband.

When the luckless man saw the strangers coming over

the crags, he took refuge in his house. Using cross-bows, the attackers fired blazing bolts into the thatch of the dwelling, and when the doomed man ran out, they shot him through the neck. They then rowed across to the island and cut off his head.

The Lord of Reay placed the head on a platter and took it to the widow: 'Now, Madam, will you stay with me?'

The loch where this incident took place is still known as Loch a'Mhuirt, 'the murder loch', and I never pass by without thinking of this grim tale. To the west of Loch a'Mhuirt is Loch na Mnatha, 'the mother's loch'. The Lord of Reay gave it to the widow as consolation for the loss of her husband.

These were hard, bitter days for common folk. Life was cheap and the laird was the law. On a rocky prominence 60 ft above the sea near Wick, stand the ruins of Sinclair and Girnigoe Castles, ancient homes of the Earls of Caithness. From these grim fastnesses, self-seeking, pragmatic men ruled their domains with harsh justice and feudal authority.

During the middle of the sixteenth century, George Sinclair, a man of boundless energy and ambition, was the fourth Earl, and an important figure in both local and national affairs. Although it was never proven, it was likely that he arranged the murder of his neighbours, the Earl and Countess of Sutherland.

The hapless couple were poisoned while staying at their hunting lodge near Helmsdale. Isobel Sinclair, a servant in the house and a relative of the Earl of Caithness, was convicted of the crime, but she escaped execution by hanging herself the night before her officially planned demise.

The Earl of Caithness moved quickly to obtain guardianship of the young successor to the Sutherland lands and rapidly married him off to his thirty-year-old daughter, Barbara.

Convinced that his avaricious father-in-law planned to have him murdered also, the young Earl fled to Morayshire. In a towering rage, George Sinclair ordered his son John, Master of Caithness, to visit Sutherland and teach the inhabitants a lesson they would not forget in a hurry.

Consequently, in company with the chief of the Strathnaver MacKays, John marched south and laid siege to the town of Dornoch. After many weeks John managed to secure concessions from the townsfolk and hostages against their continued good behaviour. But the old Earl was made of sterner stuff. He wanted neither hostages nor concessions, but rather Sutherland itself. He refused to ratify the agreement and ordered his son to put the hostages to death and burn the town.

John refused to do so and fled to Reay to escape his father's wrath. He married MacKay's sister. After some years, and many pleading letters from his father, he agreed to visit him to make up their differences. Wisely, he left his family behind, for the moment he had entered the castle, he was seized and flung into the dungeon, where he was to remain '... keiped in miserable captivity for the space of seaven yeirs.'

During his captivity, John managed to strangle his younger brother, who used to visit him to gloat. Eventually, the Earl gave orders for his son to be starved. After a week the captive was given salt pork to eat, but when he begged for water, none was given. John Sinclair died in a tormented agony of pain and raging thirst.

On the death of George Sinclair, the murdered John's son fell heir to the title. His first act was, personally, to murder his father's two gaolers.

I was born and brought up in Edinburgh and attended the Royal High School, one of the oldest places of learning in Scotland. Here, too, the Caithness Sinclairs had disrupted life in both classroom and town. The new Earl sent his son William to Edinburgh to be educated. In 1594, Sinclair organised the pupils in a 'barring-out' of masters and staff over some long forgotten grievance. When Bailie John McMorane and the Town's officers arrived, they were refused admission, and so they attempted to batter down the door.

William Sinclair, from an upstairs window, called upon them to stop, saying that if they did not, he would shoot the Bailie. No one believed that the boy would carry out his threat and the battering continued. Sinclair, following the instincts of a long line of head-strong ancestors, without hesitation, shot the Bailie through the head. His only punishment was expulsion from the school and banishment to Sinclair and Girnigoe.

My wife and I often visit the castles, and on wild days we seek shelter in the grim ruins. From the heights we watch green foam-fringed waves beating upon black rocks far below and listen to the constant cry of wheeling gulls. At times, it seems that other, more human, cries are borne on the wind.

The Earls of Caithness never did manage to lay their hands upon Sutherlandshire, but the memories linger. When I have fished the Helmsdale I have often found myself wondering what other tales and dark deeds its clear waters conceal.

George Sutherland has fished the Helmsdale for the past thirty years, and in April, 1984, he landed his ten-thousandth salmon. The Helmsdale is probably the finest salmon river in the north. Each season more than 3,000 salmon are caught on rod and line.

George started as a gillie when the Belgrave Arms Hotel at Helmsdale needed an extra man for a week. George was given a trial, and has been there ever since. But it is not a full-time job. Gillies are on full pay only from 1 March to the end of the season. George used to go to sea during the winter months, but few vessels remain in Helmsdale harbour, so things are never very easy now.

George told me that there were times on the Helmsdale when you could throw your cap into the river and a salmon would rise to it—'... when even the greatest duffer in the world—and we get them—will hook fish if he can put his line out!'

A few years ago, George was asked if he would take out a beginner and try to get him a fish. The first day they landed 25 salmon and thought it was a record. Next day they took 32 more. During the week the young man had 39 fish to his own rod, including two caught on the same cast. George saw the first fish take the fly, but when he landed it he was surprised to find another on the tail fly. They weighed 8 lb and 6 lb. By the end of the week, the young gentleman thought that salmon fishing was the finest sport ever devised.

The last day I had on the Helmsdale ended in a blank, due mostly to my inexperience and a howling gale. The river is often affected by high winds, and George sometimes has to cast for his gentlemen, or ladies, if they are to have any chance at all.

Recently, fishing with Mrs Fitzjohn, George would make the cast and then hand the rod to his lady. Nevertheless, between them they caught 14 fish. It's all part of the service, says George.

He seems able to redeem the most hopeless day. A lady hooked her first salmon and George watched helplessly as the fish stripped off line, backing and all, before he could calm her down enough to listen to his advice.

When, eventually, the line broke, the lady began to sob with frustration. George threw down his net and sprinted downstream to a bend in the river. He was just in time to see the backing going down the pool. Splashing in, he managed to grab the backing and bring the fish under control. Patiently, carefully, he coaxed the salmon back upstream, re-threaded the backing on to the rod, and tied it to the reel. The lady wound in and, after a struggle, landed a beautiful, clean-run fish of 15 lb.

George's strangest story is even harder to believe, but he has plenty of credible witnesses. He was fishing with a party of young folk, including Ms Sabrina Guinness, who had never caught a salmon.

He set Ms Guinness to fish in a pool known as the Gravelly Pool, and soon she hooked a fish. In her excitement, she clapped her hand on the line and the fish broke it. When they rejoined the main party, an argument developed with the young lads as to which had really broken, the line or the cast.

A new cast was made up and George took the young lady back to the Gravelly Pool. Watching carefully, George saw the line stop and said: 'Now, tighten.' Up came the line previously broken. The tail-fly of the new cast had caught the dropper of the old one. The salmon was still there and was duly landed.

But it is not always so easy. In 1980 George was fishing with a Mr Kelton. They started at 7 o'clock in the morning in the Marl Pool. By 9.45 they had risen 108 fish and managed to catch only one. All down the pool, the water was broken by the tails, backs and fins of rising salmon, and they watched as fish after fish followed the fly only to turn away at the last moment, regardless of the pattern offered.

'That's what makes fishing such an interesting sport', said George. 'You never can really tell what will happen. There are no certainties, but my job as a gillie is to lower the odds. You see, I keep an accurate record of every fish caught on my beat. Each day I note down the water temperature, water-level, air temperature, weather conditions, wind strength and direction; which fly the fish take; the depth at which the fish are lying; how they come to the fly; and whereabouts in the pools they take. So you'll understand that I know my river very well indeed and I can put my gentlemen in just the right spot, where they are most likely to catch fish. What more can a gillie do?'

Not much, I thought—other than catch the fish for them, and where would be the fun in that?

One of the most common surnames in Sutherland is Sutherland, which can be confusing at times. Ack and Hughie Sutherland are not related to George Sutherland, but both have worked on the Helmsdale and at Berriedale for most of their lives.

Ack is at present head-keeper on the Berriedale Estate, and his brother, Hughie, has recently retired from gillieing on the Helmsdale. Hughie lives in a small cottage north of Berriedale. Antlers hang over the front door and the house stands close to the A9, looking out over the North Sea.

Hughie is a heavily-built octogenarian with a ready smile and fine sense of humour. Most of his working life has been on the hill, rather than the river, and he was employed by Sir Anthony Nutting, who had six estates in the north.

Hughie Sutherland started work as a keeper when he was eighteen, and he gillied on Loch Monar when Major Stirling let the property each year. The head-keeper was a Mr Flemming. Hughie stalked there with the late Duke of Portland's father, from Park Lodge.

He also worked at Tomintoul in the days of Colonel Haig, and he recalls that 200 brace of grouse to six guns, walking up, was common. The Colonel was strict and kept everyone walking in line abreast, watching as closely as a drill-sargeant on parade.

Hughie remembers one day when another keeper was following behind with a pony to collect the shot birds. The man was about a quarter-of-a-mile back and kept missing heaps of birds. Hughie told the head-keeper and was dispatched to tell the fellow to come nearer. It was to no avail.

'Not on your life! I'll get shot!' he complained.

Eventually, the head-keeper himself had to tell him to move forward.

Now there was a Frenchman on the hill that day, a Mr Du Pont, and he was on the end of the line. A bird got up and Du Pont swung right round and fired at it. The next thing Hughie knew was that the horse was up on its hind-legs, screaming, and the man was running in circles, yelling and holding his backside.

Fortunately, no great damage had been done to man or beast. The Frenchman was most apologetic, offering his hip-flask to the wounded keeper and peeling notes from his pocket-book as fast as he could go, which quietened things down and ended the matter. Hughie heard later that the Colonel gave the man a lecture the likes of which he would never forget.

At the top of the Helmsdale River is Loch Achnamoine. This used to be one of the most productive fishing areas. In the summer months, particularly, the loch held hundreds of salmon, and if you knew where to look, sport could be fast and furious. One evening, returning from the hill, Hughie was skirting the south shore of the loch and noticed a shelf under the water close to the bank.

Looking more closely, he saw dozens of salmon lying just under the shelf. Next day, after hours of fruitless effort in the river, he suggested to his gentleman that they try the loch. The gentleman and his wife were due to leave the following morning, and Hughie was anxious that he should take something back south, because he had been fishless all week but was still very keen.

The lady did not fish, but sat in the car reading a book while Hughie got the boat ready: 'Great readers, some of those ladies.' Hughie rowed across the loch and manoeuvred the boat until it was within easy casting distance of the ledge. 'Now, Sir, just you cast in and drop your fly about a foot from yon black edge you're seeing.'

The gentleman did as he was instructed and placed the fly perfectly. As soon as he started to draw it towards the boat a salmon rushed from under the ledge and grabbed it.

To avoid disturbing the other fish, Hughie rowed to the middle of the loch to let the gentleman play the fish. This took some time, because the gentleman was fishing with a light trout rod, but eventually the fish was safely landed.

Hughie rowed back in and the gentleman cast again. Another fine fish was soon in the boat. By three o'clock they had seven fish, and the little Black Doctor on the end of the cast was almost bitten bare.

The fish were laid out on the lawn of Navidale House Hotel, Hughie was given a fine bottle of malt whisky, and everyone was clamouring to fish the loch next day. But, as is so often the case in salmon-fishing, not another fish came off the loch all week.

Hughie's brother, Ack Sutherland, is the present head-keeper at Berriedale, in Caithness. Towards the end of the eighteenth century the estate was in the hands of that great agriculturist, Sir John Sinclair, who introduced the hardy Border sheep to Caithness, which sparked off the Highland Clearances. The present owner is Lady Anne Bentinck. The Berriedale lands include some of the most dramatic and varied scenery in the north, with the tumbling little Berriedale River flowing from the stark heights of Morven and the Scarabens by tree-clad banks and rocky gorge to the sea.

The narrow road to the lodge winds uphill through ancient trees and round dangerous corners. On one particularly bad bend is a warning notice: 'Watch out for Anne'. I'm told this caution applies as much today as it did when Lady Anne was a small child, although for entirely different reasons!

Ack Sutherland has worked on the Berriedale Estate since he left school, and he knows the hills 'better than I know my own face'. The late Duke of Portland was a keen stalker, and it was largely due to his efforts that Berriedale gained such renown as a deer-forest.

During his years at Berriedale, the Duke shot more than 1,000 stags, and the dining-room of the lodge held a great display of heads. In the 1920s the Duke decided to have them photographed. Three separate pictures had to be taken to include them all.

Unfortunately, while the photographs were being

processed, the dining-room was burned down. The staff were ordered to try to save as much of the furniture and fittings as possible. But the Duke was more interested in his collection of stags' heads than antique tables and paintings. By the time the fire was put out, the lawns surrounding the building were scattered with stags' heads, torn from the walls and hurled through the windows to safety.

The Duke was most anxious that they should be remounted in exactly the same position as before, and he spent hours wandering round, shifting one head here and placing another there. Meantime, the photographs, taken before the blaze, had been developed and printed. It was discovered that the Duke had placed all the heads in exactly their original positions.

Ack never really wanted to be anything other than a keeper, and he takes great pride in his work. He has stalked to Prince Charles and describes him as being a first-class shot.

Over the years he has worked with many other fine sportsmen, but today, shooting and stalking is dominated more and more by parties from the Middle East. Recently a group arrived on the hill by helicopter, complete with body-guards and gunsmith. Ack spoke to the gunsmith who told him that when the Egyptians first came to his shop, they spent thousands of pounds on guns and equipment.

'Have you a large business?' they had asked.

'No, but I soon will have!' the gunsmith had replied.

One of the gentlemen stepped from the helicopter in flowing white robes, open-toed sandals and a white skull-cap. Ack said he looked like a ghost as he walked over the hill, but he was one of the finest shots Ack had seen.

Reaching Berriedale has not always been easy. In the Duke of Portland's book, *Fifty Years and More of Sport in Scotland*, is an account of what the journey was like in 1863. Lord Galway relates:

'There were no sleeping berths in these days, or even good night trains, so, on Wednesday, August 5th, we went by train to Perth, where we stopped for the night. Next morning we left Perth at 9.20 and arrived in Aberdeen at about 12.30, where we got some soup and drove across to the other station, from which we went in an appalling slow train by Inverramsay, and arrived at Inverness at 7 o'clock. The chaff was that the train occasionally stopped for the guard or engine-driver to plant his potatoes. We rested at Inverness the next day and drove down with Alfred Denison in the afternoon to see him fish the Ness Pool, in which last year he hooked a salmon which he estimated at quite 50 lb, but, after playing him all night through, the tackle broke.

'We left Inverness on the Saturday morning at 10 by train to Alves station, whence, after waiting an hour we came to Burghead, where we embarked on a little steamer, the *Heather Bell*. It began to blow and the sea got rough, and I was very glad when we got to land, especially as about half-way across the Captain came to me and asked me if my Father could not give him a lodge-keeper's place, as he expected every day that the old ship would go to the bottom and he would be drowned! We arrived at Little Ferry at 6.30, and drove off at once to Golspie, where we got some dinner. We started from there about 8.30, changed at Helmsdale, and at last arrived at the house at Langwell at 12.30, where they had begun to despair of our arriving'.

One of the Duke's friends, Chandy Pole, claimed to have kept a diary of a journey north made in 1895. For me, his caustic comments sum up all the dubious pleasures of travelling. The contents of the diary are brief and to the point:

First night.	Arrived.	Whisky good.
Second night.	do	Whisky moderate.
Third night.	do	Whisky bad.

Fourth night.	do	Whisky d— bad.
Fifth night.	do	Whisky again d— bad,
		and barmaid d— ugly.
		Will never come back here again.

Even today, travel by rail and road to the far north is a major expedition. We live three hours north of Inverness and to get anywhere involves many an unwelcome blast from a raucous alarm clock, long yawns, and an early breakfast. In my opinion, the recent television programme, *Great Train Journeys of the World*, missed one of the greatest—the 5.30 am Wick to Inverness, a four-and-a-half hour slog through Caithness and Sutherland to civilisation. Oh, for a helicopter then!

But a certain sense of adventure is aroused in coming north, and distance is a great barrier. Anyone venturing this far has really to be determined, so most of our visitors are of the best kind of sportsmen and fishers—and they don't come much more determined than them.

Berriedale was, and is, a superb sporting estate. Records of stags killed on Langwell and Braemore between 1880 to 1932 amount to 4,720, ninety each season. One of the best stags ever shot was killed by Sir Ronald Graham at Braemore on 21 August, 1927. The span of the horns was $36\frac{7}{8}$ inches inside and $39\frac{1}{8}$ inches outside.

One of the most memorable of the Duke's stalks occurred on 10 October, 1925, in company with Ivy Tichfield:

'We came across a very fine Royal Stag, which we called Trafadd from his generally being in the part of the forest known by that name. We stalked him every day for no less than six days. From the first two or three days we found it impossible to get a shot at him, but on the fourth day the stag left the ground on which we usually found him and went to the Scarabens. We followed him there and, having climbed above him, I thought I was going to have a shot; but bad luck to it, just as I got into position to shoot, a heavy storm of rain and sleet disturbed the stag, and I could only get a long shot of about 250 yds, which I missed.

'The next day, when I was again accompanied by Ivy and my grand-daughter, Anne, Trafadd was back on his original ground. We had a tremendous crawl on very flat ground, but could not get nearer than a quarter-of-a-mile from him.

'On the sixth day we found him again, and stalked him all day long, the wind being in the west. Towards evening, having the wind turned more to the north, Ralph Armstrong said to me, "We shall likely get a shot at him soon." Just as we were proceeding to stalk him another big stag appeared, and the two of them had a tremendous fight above Braigh Na H-Eaglaise Wood, opposite the Putting Stone. Ralph said to me, "Now it all depends on the result of this fight, and whether 'Trafadd' wins or not."

'Fortunately for us, Trafadd won, resumed possession of the hinds, and disappeared into the wood. We then managed to get above them and I caught a glimpse of him below us, nearly on the bank of the river. I took a quick shot and heard the thud of the bullet, when Ralph whispered in my ear, "And so ends Trafadd." We went down the hill, and there the poor fellow was lying, stone dead. Ivy picked up a stone, and gave it to me. I had a little plate put on with the name Trafadd and the date of his death.

'I have made a special record of this stalk, because I believe we must have walked at least 50 miles in pursuit of the stag; in any case, whatever the distance may have been, it was most destructive to Ivy's shoes—she walked the heel off one and the sole off the other. Trafadd had a fairly good Royal head and weighed 20 stone.'

My wife, Ann, and I spend many hours walking over the hills and moors of Caithness and Sutherland.

Frequently, we surprise herds of wild red deer, and the beasts stare unflinchingly at our unwelcome presence before bounding off. Little do they realise the honesty of our intent. But I suppose, after so many years of relentless pursuit, they have learned the hard way that 'two legs' are bad news.

The far north of Scotland is one of the last great wilderness areas of Europe. It is still full of marvellous salmon rivers, trout lochs, grouse moors and deer forests. It is a very special land, remote and beautiful where, for the price of a few miles' walk, you are master of all you survey.

Above all, the visitor will find courtesy, humour, knowledge and help from some of nature's finest folk in the gillies and keepers of this far and remote land.

CHAPTER 9

One that
got away on Tay

We camped at Inver, near the cathedral town of Dunkeld
in Perthshire. Tents were pitched, kitchens constructed,
haversacks unpacked. Then I made for the river. My first
sight of the Tay is as clear today as it was then, thirty-three
years ago, as an eager Boy Scout: the broad stream, tree-
lined banks, deep pools, mysterious swirls and eddies, the
splash of rising trout, and the sudden dash of a salmon
moving upstream.

I fell in love with Perthshire on that first visit, and I have been captivated by the county ever since. For an unforgettable two weeks we explored the surrounding countryside: expeditions were made up the rocky River Bran to swim in pools below the Hermitage, and a raft was constructed to ferry the Patrol over the Tay at the start of an adventure hike.

Two of the younger boys couldn't swim, so I swam the river first, towing a rope. This was attached to the raft for safety and everyone was hauled across dry-shod and secure. We struck off northwards, through the trees, up the steep slope of Craig a Barns. On the moors we headed for Rotmell Loch, then over Deuchary Hill to Loch na Beinne. We travelled in a straight line, and when our way was barred by crags or cliffs, ropes were uncoiled and obstacles scaled.

That night we slept under the stars by Loch Ordie. As the soft summer darkness enclosed us, hundreds of bats whisked from ruined buildings, making the air loud with whirring wings. We lay on beds of heather and listened to the noises of the Perthshire night: water lapping on loch shore; curlews crying down the hill; the plaintiff piping of plovers; the wind rustling the rowans, over recumbent bodies.

Next morning we washed in Loch Ordie and then walked through Drubuie Woods to reed-fringed Loch of Craiglush. On the way a dappled roe-deer rose, startled, from the forest floor. I saw my first capercailzie, turkey-like and ridiculous, swaying on a thin branch in a pine tree. A jay swept colourfully by. Wrens and finches flitted down 'with tiny-eyed caution, jerkily to eat', and the woods were full of birdsong.

I had just started fishing and I had brought my trout rod with me. It was an ancient greenheart, 11 ft long and creaking, given to me by a friend of my father. I was still trying to master the art of casting, but one evening, after supper, I walked upstream from Inver and fished the pool below where the new bridge now carries the A9 over the Tay.

As any angler will know, certain moments are remembered with such clarity that even shades of colour in the water, the moment of the fly landing and the fish rising can be instantly recalled. The fish I saw that evening was the largest I had ever seen, a salmon of some 15 lb. Trees lined the bank and made casting difficult, but I persevered and eventually, after a great deal of cursing and tree-climbing, managed to get my single fly into the middle of the pool.

Fly and cast landed on the surface in a coiled heap, and my heart stopped as the huge fish rose lazily to take the size sixteen Grouse and Claret. I was transfixed by a combination of fear and excitement as my reel screamed— and my cast broke. If ever I had had a single doubt about my desire to become an angler, it was dispelled there and then. I never speed over that bridge now without feeling again all the painful pleasure of that glorious moment.

The most famous glorious moment on the Tay, however, happened sixteen years before I was born. On 7 October, 1922, Miss G. W. Ballantine caught the largest salmon ever taken on rod and line in Britain. The fish weighed 64 lb, was 54 inches long, 28½ inches in girth, and had a head 12 inches long and tail 11 inches long.

Miss Ballantine was the daughter of the gillie on the Glendelvine Beat, and the fish was hooked in the Boat Pool. The Duke of Portland described the event thus:

'I understand that her father was rowing home in the evening with a large spinning bait trailing behind the boat. The bait was suddenly seized and Ballantine told his daughter (who was in the boat) to catch hold of the rod. She did so and kept the point up. The fish ran downstream, passing under Caputh Bridge, when Ballantine and his daughter landed on some shingle on the right bank of the river about quarter-of-a-mile

141

below the bridge. There they landed the fish, which proved to be the heaviest fish ever killed by rod and line on the Tay.'

We men have been trying ever since to better Miss Ballantine's feat, and few tried harder or had more opportunity than the late Duke. In 1914 the Duke of Portland became tenant of Burnmouth, Catholes, Benchill, Redgorton and Upper and Lower Scone beats on the Tay. He fished the river from 1922 until 1932, and during that time he and his guests landed nearly 1,300 salmon.

In 1922, a good season, one of the Duke's guests, Barker Carr, had a record day on Lower Stanley when he caught 17 salmon. The heaviest fish weighed 30 lb while the smallest weighed 8 lb.

'On 9 March the river was still high, but was falling. Wind, south-east and cold. I caught nearly all the fish on a large Black Dog or a Dusty Miller. I killed two small fish in the Washing Pool, and the others in Pitlochry Pool. The total weight of these fish was 276 lb, with an average weight of 16 lb.'

That season, during forty days' fishing, 189 salmon were caught by the Duke, Barker Carr and their gillie, Arthur Ager. The average weight was 17½ lb.

In 1930, on Lower Stanley, the Duke reported:

'On March 11 I was fortunate enough to kill 13 fish in three-and-a-half hours on Lower Stanley: 12 of these fish were caught between 2 pm and 6.30 pm. Nearly all of them were taken spinning with a Golden Sprat. The total weight was 211 lb, average weight 16 and one-quarter pounds. It is only right that I should mention that the same number of fish, i.e. 13, were killed on the following day by a Mr Mathewson of Dundee on the same water. Mr Mathewson's catch was 13 fish which weighed 249 lb, with an average weight of 19 lb.'

But the most remarkable record from the Duke's fishing diary concerns not the Tay, but the famous Alten River in Norway:

'No less than 684 salmon were killed between June 25 and July 22, 1926, on the River Alten in Norway. All these salmon were caught on the fly, and in addition to this number of salmon, 75 grilse were also caught. Of this bag Cis Hamilton killed 208 fish, the Duke of Westminster 173 fish, Sir Joseph Laycock 154 fish, Mr Corbet 107 fish, and the officers of the Duke of Westminster's yacht 42 fish, making a total of 684 fish which weighed 15,720 lb = 7 tons, with an average weight of 23 lb. One night, between 7.30 pm and 9 am the Duke of Westminster killed 33 fish which averaged 24 lb.'

Today, one can only speculate on what was done with seven tons of salmon. Great fishermen they may have been, but great sportsmen ...?

The Duke of Portland described how he disproved the theory that fish lose weight after being caught:

'I had a fish which I caught in the Tay weighed at 11 o'clock—weight, 20 lb. It was again weighed at luncheon-time—weight, 20 lb; again at tea-time—weight, 20 lb; and again when I got home, it weighed 20 lb. To complete the test, next morning it again weighed 20 lb. My dear old friend, Major Barker Carr, then said: "Do not waste any more time weighing the damn fish, let's have it for dinner!" '

Although the Tay has never boasted such enormous rod-and-line catches as the Alten, it still remains one of the most consistently excellent salmon waters.

One of the best beats is Cargill (in 1982 1,000 salmon were caught, and the average is almost always more than 500 fish), and one of the best gillies is Colin Leslie, the man who looks after Cargill.

During his years at Cargill, Colin has caught twenty fish of more than 40 lb to his own rod. His heaviest salmon was a fish of 56½ lb, which took nearly an hour-and-a-half to land. It was 'a big autumn cock fish with a great kype on him'. But the salmon he remembers with most pleasure was a springer of 46½ lb that fought like a demon until Colin's arms and back ached as never before and he despaired of seeing the fish on the bank. 'It was covered in sea-lice and like a bar of pure silver.'

Colin was born at Ruthven, on the banks of the River Isla. His father used to take him and his brother up the river, and it was there, by Inverquiech, Dryloch and Dillavaird, that Colin caught his first fish. He remembers the Isla after spawning time, '... as though the bottom of the river had been ploughed, so many salmon crowded the redds. Now, there's hardly a salmon to be seen.'

Colin joined the Royal Navy when he left school, and later, after the war, had a spell managing a farm. But his real love was for fishing, and he has gillied at Cargill for more than thirty years. He is a man of medium height, round-faced, with a ready smile and a mischievous twinkle in his eyes. When I telephoned to seek help and advice, he readily agreed to talk, and we arranged to meet in the fishing-hut.

I arrived on a cold February morning, snow still sprinkling the fields and the wind knife-like, cutting to the bone. Colin was sitting by the fire. The walls of the hut were covered with an array of photographs of gentlemen who had fished with him over the years: Colonel Hardy (of whom Winston Churchill is reputed to have remarked: "That rare bird, a Socialist millionaire."); Sir Francis de Guingand, Field-Marshal Montgomery's Chief of Staff at Alamein during the Second World War; Nelson D. Rockefeller, the American financier, and his son, John. It was a gallery of famous names, united in their passion for fishing.

Colin still has the tip he received from Nelson Rockefeller, who came to fish for a week. They took a good number of fish and at the end of their visit Colin ran down to the gate and held it open for them as they left. The car stopped and Nelson D. wound down the window and thanked Colin for all his hard work and for making their week so enjoyable. He drew a large brown envelope from his pocket and handed it to Colin: 'Here's a little something for all your trouble, Colin.'

Colin hurried back to the fishing-hut, curious and excited, wondering what the great financier had left him. When he opened the envelope, he found that it contained a single ten-shilling note, nothing else. After his initial surprise, Colin just laughed and laughed. 'No wonder he was a very wealthy man', he said. 'But I wish he could have seen the look on my face when I opened his envelope!'

The photographs and Colin's fishing diary are truly international: Chinese, Indians, Swiss, Dutch, French, Americans, Arabs, Australians and Maoris, anglers and 'hopefuls' from all over the world. Colin has long since lost count of the number of gentlemen and their families he has taught to fish; the hooks he has extracted from humans and animals; the sopping-wet fishermen he has hauled from the river; the courteous and not-so-courteous; the good, the bad and the ugly.

Among the latter, Colin particularly remembers a party from Blackpool: 'All loud-mouthed, loud-suited and long-winded, with big rings on their fingers and big cars on the bank.'

It was one of those days when everything was just perfect, and by finishing time, 5.30 pm, 50 salmon were on the bank. Everything was kept, indiscriminately: hen fish heavy with spawn, foul-hooked fish, anything on which they could lay their hands. They refused to stop and, in spite of all Colin said, thrashed on. All the fish they caught were to be sold to hotels in Lancashire. It was more

145

business than fishing. Eventually Colin went ashore and telephoned the Factor, who came down and chased them from the river. They were never allowed back.

The older Colin becomes, the fewer sportsmen he meets. In the 'old days' a very different sort of gentlemen used to fish the river. For forty years a surgeon from Leicester fished with Colin at Cargill. If a big hen fish, ready to spawn, was caught, it was carefully put back into the river. A foul-hooked salmon was always released. If a good few fish were caught in the morning, then that was the end of the day's sport.

'It's not like that today, believe me', Colin said. 'They're at it from dawn to dusk and hardly a fly-rod among them, raking away at the bottom with lumps of iron. At times the river is red and blue from the dye coming out of their shrimps and prawns. They're interested in telling their friends back home that they've been salmon-fishing in Scotland, and that they hooked a fish. It's me that hooks the fish for them when we're harling. Many of them shouldn't be let near a river. They'd be as well buying a salmon from the fishmonger than wasting my time with their daft antics!

'Any idiot can catch salmon with prawns or lures, but proper salmon-fishing is fly-fishing. It always has been and, as far as I'm concerned, always will be.'

One group of four gentlemen who fished with Colin recently organised themselves so efficiently that their fishing was constant, and so was Colin's work. Two would go out in the boat with Colin in the morning while the other two fished from the bank. The bank-fishers would have lunch early, so that when the boat party came ashore to eat, they could leap in immediately and start fishing. For two days the only respite Colin managed was a quick bite of a sandwich between bank and shore and a rest from the oars when motoring back upstream to begin the next drift.

To rectify matters, on the third morning, Colin waited

until they had got themselves sorted out, two scuttling away up the bank, the other pair waiting impatiently in the boat. Then he locked the fishing-hut door. At the end of the morning Colin could see the bank-fishers stamping about, peering into the hut, shouting and waving for the key. But Colin said nothing and kept the boat at the bottom of the Beat until his gentlemen finally noticed: 'We'll go in for lunch now, if you please.'

There were two long faces when they arrived back, but when Colin unlocked the fishing-hut, they fell on their lunch like hungry wolves and within minutes were sitting in the boat, demanding to be taken out.

'Now, just look here, gentlemen', said Colin, 'I'm having a break and my lunch in peace today. The fish will still be there in half-an-hour, so you'll just have to be patient.'

It did no good. The gentlemen groused and girned so much that after ten minutes Colin abandoned all hope of rest and took them out for the sake of peace and quiet.

The Isla enters the Tay upstream from Cargill and Colin's beat is fast-flowing and wide. When I arrived, Colin pointed out the Isla water, coloured and brown, flowing down the east side of the river, and the Tay water, clean and clear, running down the Ballathie shore.

The Isla was in spate after heavy rain, and looking at the fast-flowing waters, I was reminded that it was in the Tay that I came as close as I ever want to come to drowning. It was on the home-made raft that I mentioned earlier. The excellent vessel had been constructed out of two empty 40-gallon drums by my friend William Calder and myself. Before leaving Dunkeld and returning to Edinburgh, we decided to take the raft into the middle of the river, dive off, and let it go—a sort of back-to-front Viking funeral.

It nearly became our funeral, for the Tay was in spate and coming down in a torrent. With the thoughtlessness of youth, we launched the raft and quickly found ourselves being swept uncontrollably downstream towards Dunkeld bridge. After a quick consultation, we dived into the river and struck out for the shore. As the water tugged and pulled me downstream, I felt the beginnings of panic. Trying to keep calm, I swam as strongly as I could and, after what seemed an eternity, grabbed the roots of a tree overhanging the bank and hauled myself ashore.

I struggled upright and saw William hauling himself on to the bank further downstream. The distance we had swum from raft to shore was only a few yards, yet we had been swept hundreds of yards downstream, almost to the bridge.

I asked Colin Leslie if he had experienced difficulties with gentlemen falling into the river. He confessed that some of his gentlemen fell into the water all too easily after taking too much early-morning refreshment. Apart from being dangerous, Colin explained that it wasted a lot of good fishing time. So to keep his gentlemen both safe and sober, Colin has devised a simple method of dealing with the situation. If he suspects there may be difficulties, he simply keeps the boat in shallow water and lets them tumble in and out to their hearts' content until they come to their senses and behave. 'No matter what happens, you always have to look after your gentlemen.'

One morning, when Colin was fishing with the retired Chief Constable of Dundee, the river was a good five feet higher than normal. Colin had warned the gentleman of the danger of standing too near the edge of the river, but to no avail. One moment the Chief Constable was there, casting; the next, Colin saw him take a beautiful header straight into seven feet of freezing water. The bank had given way. The water temperature was below 38 degrees Fahr, and it took a good hour in front of the fishing-hut fire to dry out the gentleman. But if Colin had not been there, and acted quickly, the ex-policeman would have retired for good.

Sir Francis de Ginguid also took a tumble into the river. The General had gone up to the railway bridge for a few casts while Colin prepared the boat. Colin heard a great splash. 'Oh, the General is into a fish', he thought, but when he arrived on the scene, net ready, he found the General scrambling about on his hands and knees, spluttering and cursing, trying to get out of the river.

'What the blazes are you laughing at, man?' roared the General. He dragged himself to his feet and, water dripping from soaking clothes, marched up the bank to stop, red-faced and furious, two inches from Colin's nose. 'I just hope that I'm around the day you fall in. I'll laugh my damned head off!'

Colin and the General became firm friends, and Sir Francis fished Cargill regularly until his recent death.

Colonel Hardy's boatman, Willie Cowans, on the Ballathie side was another great character and famous Tay gillie. Willie had served eighteen years, man and boy, in the Cameron Highlanders, and Sir Francis wanted to meet the old man. Colin introduced them:

'Hey, Willie, here's a gentleman who says that the Cameron Highlanders were no bloody use!'

Willie had never lost the habit of keeping his hair very short, and he shook his head, his eyes starting from his outraged face.

'Then you don't know what the devil you're talking aboot, maun. Whit mob were you with?'

'I was with the Green Howards', the General replied. Willie roared with derision.

'Green Howards? Never bloody heard of them!'

The General had good sport and great fun over the years, and caught more than his fair share of large Tay salmon. But the biggest fish Colin ever saw rose one morning when he was fishing with a Mrs Morris. The lady, the wife of the founder of the Morris Crane Company, had fished all over the world, including Norway, Sweden and Canada. Her largest fish was a Pacific salmon of 68 lb caught in the sea off the Canadian west coast. Colin had seen enough salmon to be able accurately to assess the weight of a fish.

The big Tay salmon jumped clean out of the water about five yards from the boat.

'I'll never forget it. My stomach took a turn and I looked at Mrs Morris and said, "Did you see that, Madam? What do you think of that fish?" '

They both saw the whole fish and estimated it to be about six feet long and three feet deep, with a tail like a coal-shovel. Their best estimate of its weight was close to 100 lb.

'I never saw another fish like it, before or since. What a fright I got! I wondered what was coming out of the water. Oh, I wish I'd hooked him!'

Like most gillies and anglers on the Tay, Colin feels that the quality of salmon-fishing is in an almost irreversible decline. His main criticism is of the management of the river and the introduction of the hydro-electric dam at Pitlochry. In the days before the dam was built, Colin used to fish the Tummel and catch as many as 14 salmon before lunch, all on the fly. Now the fish are very few.

The salmon-ladder seems to be well-designed and successful, but in practice, Colin is not so sure. He feels that kelts, and particularly smolts, have great difficulty in finding their way down to the main river.

'There's one part of the dam where gulls collect and feed ravenously on smolts, and last season only 3,000 fish were counted through.'

Neither is Colin persuaded that electric-fishing methods operated by river superintendents in the spawning grounds have been sufficiently tested with regards to their overall safety.

'Has anyone investigated what effect electric stunners have on salmon eggs, and what damage they may cause to other river life—flies and freshwater snails?'

The truth of these matters is always hard to establish. People have probably been complaining that the river is not as good as it was for as long as salmon have run the Tay. However, this time there does seem to be grave cause for concern if the Tay is to maintain its position as one of the great salmon rivers of the world.

A few details from past records illustrate the point. In 1910, from 22 March until 23 April, during twenty-three days' fishing, the Duke and Duchess of Bedford and the Marquess of Tavistock took 151 salmon. The Duke of Portland, during the years he fished the Tay, recorded the following results:

1922, 189 salmon	1926, 59 salmon	1930, 93 salmon
1923, 143 salmon	1927, 133 salmon	1931, 79 salmon
1924, 40 salmon	1928, 106 salmon	1932, 34 salmon
1925, 98 salmon	1929, 81 salmon	

But then, in 1933, the Duke addressed a letter to the Press:

'Salmon Angling on the Tay
'I am afraid the following figures show the gradual deterioration of the salmon rod fishing on the two beats (Lower Stanley and Benchill) which I believe are rightly considered the best beats, during the spring season, on the lower part of the Tay.

'Between 1 March and 15 April, considered the best six weeks of the spring, the number of fish killed from 1927 up till this year was as follows:

1927, 90	1931, 58
1928, 87	1932, 33
1929, 68	1933, 25
1930, 79	

'I am told by one whose practical knowledge cannot be disputed that the number of fish taken by the rod during the so-called autumn fishing shows as great, if not greater, diminution.

'I can say that never in my experience have so few kelts been caught or seen as has been the case during this spring, which is sure proof, I think, that, comparatively speaking, few salmon ascended the Tay during 1932. I believe the reason for this decline is the excessive netting in the estuary and in the river itself. It seems a great pity to destroy "the goose that lays the golden egg" and to ruin one of the finest salmon rivers in Scotland.

'I may say that during the many seasons I have fished the beats referred to, seldom has the river kept in better order to catch fish than it was during the last six weeks, so lack of water is certainly not the reason for the very poor results.

Portland'

Now here are details from Colin Leslie's diary, forty-one years later, of fourteen days' fishing in 1974, from 30 September until 15 October:

30 Sept, 13 (best fish, 35 lb)	9 Oct, 22 (two weighing 25 lb)
1 Oct, 14	10 Oct, 14 (best fish, 26 lb)
2 Oct, 5	11 Oct, 16
3 Oct, 8	12 Oct, 26 (fish of 31 lb
4 Oct, 7	and two of 30 lb)
5 Oct, 11	14 Oct, 11
7 Oct, 10 (best fish, 28 lb)	15 Oct, 12 (best fish, 25 lb)
8 Oct, 27 (best fish, 25 lb)	

That is a total of 196 salmon in fourteen days, or 14 fish per day; and the total from Cargill for the season was 858—enough to bring a sparkle to the eye of any angler, anywhere.

It is apparent from these brief details that conditions until 1974 were not dramatically different from those in the 'good old days'. What worries present-day Tay anglers, however, is the relentless netting of the river, coupled with the uncontrolled pursuit of salmon at sea. The last ten-year average, 1974/1984, on one of the best beats of the

Tay, including the Duke of Portland's Pitlochry and Benchill Pools, fell to 375 salmon and grilse. If the days of the Bedfords, Portland, Barker Carr and Tavistock are to return, then, as Colin Leslie constantly emphasises: 'Something must be done!'

But it is hard to be sombre or too serious in Colin's company. As we were looking over the fishing diary, my eye caught a gentleman's comment: 'Ca canny, Colin!'

I asked Colin to explain. Seemingly an American gentleman had come to Cargill hoping, like so many before him, to catch his first salmon. After many hours of trying—both fishing and Colin's patience—the gentleman eventually hooked a good salmon. In his excitement he put enough strain on the poor fish to take its head off at the shoulders, and Colin yelled: 'For God's sake! Ca canny, man! Ca canny!'

When the fish was eventually landed, the American turned to Colin and enquired: 'Say, Colin, what the hell does "Ca canny" mean?'

Colin explained, and at the end of his visit the gentleman wrote in Colin's book: 'Many thanks for a super week and my first salmon. Ca canny, Colin!'

Of all the trials and tribulations a gillie has to endure, Colin remembers one with great amusement. A party of English guests arrived at the river with five large, boisterous yellow Labradors.

'There were the gentleman, his lady and these five damned dogs. God! But didn't I have to pile them all into the boat, too! No sooner were we out on the river than the lady grabbed a spinning rod mounted with a Toby and gave a great heave. But she hadn't released the bale-arm and the lure caught one of the dogs in the behind. The poor beast leapt straight out of the boat in fright, leaving the lady clutching the rod and screaming and crying while she 'played' her pet and the other dogs all dashed about barking like mad, with the gentleman trying to control them.

'It took me some time to calm them down, and I had to be very firm or they would've had the boat over and everyone swimming for their lives with all their jumping about. It took even longer to 'play' the Labrador and get him back into the boat. I got the gentleman to hold the dog's head and cut the lure out with my knife. Very grateful they were, too, including the dog, which sat at my feet for the rest of the day. But it was the best run the lady had all week. She never touched a salmon!'

Colin laughed, remembering the event, and then laughed even louder as he pointed to a picture on the wall behind me. It showed a small, busy man, proudly displaying a salmon of about 15 lb. Standing at his side was an older edition of the angler, obviously his father.

The two gentlemen were Dutchmen and the salmon was the son's first fish. Colin told me he was standing by the hut when he saw the young man hook the fish. The Dutchman kept calm and played the fish well, finally leading it to a shingle bank to beach it. That was more than could be said for his father. The little man ran up and down the river-bank as his son played the fish, shouting endless encouragement and advice at the top of his voice.

Just as the lad went to beach the fish, the father dashed into the shallows and started to try to kick the salmon ashore. The more the son yelled at his father to stop, the more the old man lashed away with his feet. Anything Colin tried to suggest was completely ignored, so he retired to the steps of the fishing-hut to see what would happen.

The father fell on the salmon, trying to trap it between his knees. As the fish shot between his legs, one of the hooks from the spinning lure caught in the seat of his pants. The father stood up, still bawling instructions and searching for the fish, which was now dangling behind him. He must have told his son to kill the salmon, for the boy sprinted to a fishing-bag, grabbed a huge priest and started to belabour his father's backside.

For every blow that landed on the salmon, three landed on his father, who shrieked and yelled as though it was himself being killed rather than the salmon. Eventually, the boy grabbed the fish by the tail and managed to get his father to sit down and keep quiet. One final blow and the salmon was dispatched, detached and photographed.

'It was the funniest thing I've seen in all my years on the river, and I thought I'd die laughing', said Colin. 'Now, every time I look at that photograph, I see them dancing about and laugh all over again.'

Although Colin Leslie spends most of his time salmon-fishing, he is equally fond of trout-fishing. I was delighted when I heard that he would be visiting Caithness later in the year to fish some of our superb trout lochs, and happy to tell him of some of my own favourite waters and to offer *my* services as gillie! However, if I were to row for a year, I could never properly repay my debt of gratitude to him for the pleasure he had given me with his stories about the Tay.

CHAPTER 10

The debatable lands, Hopetoun and Willie Drysdale

In a field by the Solway Firth, one mile west from the mouth of the River Sark, is a huge boulder known as the Lochmabonstone. It stands 7 ft 10 ins, is 18 ft 8 ins in girth and weighs about ten tons.

In ancient times the stone probably formed part of a large circle of similar stones, but of them, nothing remains. However, as recently as the nineteenth century, three stones were still standing. The local tenant-farmer, to obtain better use of the ground, ordered his staff to dig them underground. Fortunately for posterity, Lord Mansfield, the owner, appeared on the scene and stopped the operation in time to save the last stone.

But the folk of this corner of south-west Scotland have always had a reputation for taking independent action, and in times past they showed scant regard for officialdom or authority. Indeed, the Lochmabonstone was the recognised gathering place for raiding parties before they set off over the Border in search of English silver and cattle.

The stone was also a meeting-place, where Scots and English attempted to resolve their many differences. An exchange of prisoners was arranged there in 1398; and in 1448 the ever-warring Douglases and Percies fought a great battle near the Lochmabonstone, when the Percies invaded Scotland and suffered humiliating defeat for their trouble.

These were unruly times on both sides of the Border. Robbery, pillage and murder were commonplace, and according to one English writer, in 1582, Gretna Green was the home of 'Scottishe theves'.

These were the 'Debatable Lands', fought over for centuries by Scots and English. The area became a place of refuge for escaped criminals and ne'er-do-wells until, by proclamation in 1551:

'All Englishmen and Scottishmen, after this proclamation made, are and shall be free to rob, burn, spoil, slay, murder and destroy all and every such person or persons, their bodies, buildings, goods and cattle as do remain or shall inhabit upon any part of the said Debatable Land, without any redress to be made for the same.'

The problem of ownership was not solved until 1552, when, with the French Ambassador acting as arbiter, a final boundary line was agreed between the two countries. It was ratified by Decree at Jedburgh on 9 November.

One of the Commissioners appointed to attend these delicate negotiations was Sir James Douglas of Drumlanrig.

Today, his lands form part of the Buccleuch Estate, near Thornhill, in Dumfriesshire.

Drumlanrig is a magnificent pink castle, built in the seventeenth century, full of Louis XIV furniture and paintings by Rembrandt and Holbein. But in the times of the Border disputes, a harsher residence was required, and this was Morton Castle, situated a few miles away near Bellybought Hill.

Morton Castle is aggressively sited on a high promontory overlooking a loch formed by a burn being dammed to create a defensive moat. The Castle dates back to the times of David 1 (1124–1153), although the present structure was built in the sixteenth century and is now in ruins.

In the mid-1700s, when repairs were being effected to the dam wall, the loch was drained and an ancient boat was dug out of the silt. The craft was unusual in that it had been hewn from a single piece of solid wood and was shaped like an Indian canoe. The estate supplies a more modern boat today, and Morton Castle Loch is stocked with excellent brown and rainbow trout.

Thornhill is an attractive little town in the valley of the River Nith, surrounded by the green and gentle Lowther Hills. Ann and I first visited the area in the early 1960s to fish the lochs and walk on the high moors. Now, I had returned to talk to two men who had spent many years working for the estate on grouse moor and river, Walter Maxwell and Andrew Hunter.

Walter lives in a neat house on the main street of Thornhill. He is a wiry, fit man with the slow, gentle humour of south-west Scotland. When I offered him a cigarette he told me, 'I stopped smoking nearly ten years ago. I was in the garden trying to lift carrots and when I found I couldn't, I stuck my pipe in a hole in the dyke, and it's been there ever since!'

For thirty years Walter farmed the land south of Morton Castle. 'Then in 1963 the Duke asked me to be head-gillie on the Nith, and now he'll not let me go.'

Walter does less gillieing these days, although his services are always in great demand, since he knows every salmon lie on the river. Some 500 salmon are taken each year on the Estate Beat, including many of the big Solway fish known as grey-backs.

The heaviest fish Walter has caught was a salmon of 38 lb 8 oz, taken in Carronfoot Pool. 'I tried fly first without success, so I changed to a Toby spoon. Got a 12 lb fish first, then the big fellow took. The rod went *whoosh* ...! Then off he went like somebody had let the pig loose. Took me an hour and ten minutes to land him, but what a beautiful fish!'

Walter looks after up to eight rods each week and during his years on the river has met many notable anglers. I was particularly interested to learn that he had gillied for Sir Tom Hickenbotham, a name I had not heard for more than a quarter of a century. Sir Tom was Governor-General of Aden when I did my soldiering there in the late 1950s. Walter spoke highly of his ability and enthusiasm for salmon-fishing.

Colonel and Mrs Collet, of Cutty Sark Whisky, also fished with Walter, and he recounted that the Colonel would fish only with fly, catching salmon as readily in low water conditions as when the river was in flood. Colonel Collet favoured a silver-bodied fly with a hairwing and was one of the most successful rods on the river.

Surprisingly, neither Walter's father nor his own children showed any interest in fishing, but his eldest grandson is keen. Walter has delighted in introducing the boy to both salmon and trout fishing.

Apart from Morton Castle Loch, two other first-class trout waters are on the estate: Starburn Loch, to the south of Drumlanrig Castle, and Kettleton Reservoir, which lies to the north of Thornhill between Parr Hill and Nether Hill.

Kettleton was opened by the Duchess of Gloucester in 1938. Walter started stocking it about twenty years ago, and now the reservoir contains some really good trout.

In his farming days, Walter always used to leave a trout rod at the spillway and, after checking on the sheep, he would have a few casts before returning home. The waterman was also a keen fisherman, so two or three spare casts were always left under a convenient rock, ready for use.

Most Nith anglers use 12 – 14 ft rods, and Walter's own favourite is a Hardy Gold Medal 13 ft rod. He ties all his own flies and over the years has found the most successful patterns to be brown-coloured flies, although Hairy Mary and Stoat's Tail always give good results, too.

The Nith is also a fine sea-trout water, and Walter ties up red-and-brown spiders to tempt them. Recently, after his gentleman had spent a fruitless day using traditional sea-trout patterns, Walter managed to persuade him to try a spider. He made up three, by the river, and within the hour nine lovely sea-trout were on the bank.

The best months for salmon and sea-trout on the Nith are June and July, but Walter says the river is but a shadow of its former self due to over-fishing at sea and the effects of salmon disease in the 1960s.

Among the farming trophies and photographs of champion cattle that adorn his living-room walls lies Walter's pride and joy, his violin. He has been playing since he was four. His mother was a professional pianist, so he has music in his blood.

When I asked Walter if he would rather have been something other than a farmer and gillie, he replied instantly, 'Probably a musician.' But it seemed to me that he had the best of all worlds—a constant demand for his services as gillie and an equally constant demand for his skills as a fiddler at dances and other local events.

I promised Walter that next time we met we would talk about music rather than fishing. Yet somehow I doubted that the subject of salmon-fishing could be long avoided.

When I called to see Andrew Hunter, he and his family

were preparing to leave their cottage by the Nith for a new home nearby; but I was invited into the depleted sitting-room and settled by the fire with a welcoming dram.

Andrew Hunter is a large, jolly man, now in his mid-seventies. He started work on the estate in 1938 and described the late Duke as being 'a bit eighteenth century, and a very easy man to get into trouble with, and you didn't speak unless you were spoken to first'.

I asked Andrew if he still managed to get down to the river, but he told me that he had recently sold all his rods following a couple of 'accidents' on the river.

The first came when he was asked to take two of the shooting guests out on the river. Andrew took them to the Long Straight Pool by Malcolmflat Wood. It is an excellent pool, but to fish it properly, the angler has to wade. Andrew waded out to show his gentleman the only dangerous part of the pool, a deep pot marked by a large rock just under the surface. The water was dirty, and before he knew what had happened, Andrew had fallen straight into the pot and his gentleman had the greatest difficulty getting him out again.

The second accident, and the last straw, came while he was fishing for sea-trout a few months ago. In the excitement of hooking and playing a good fish late at night, Andrew fell in again. With his waders full of water, and his hat still firmly pulled down, he struggled long and hard to get to his knees and scramble ashore.

That was quite enough for his long-suffering wife and family, and Andrew decided to remove temptation and to sell off his tackle.

'I was frustrated that day, I can tell you, but it had to be done. I don't go near the water these days. As likely as not I'd fall in again!'

Andrew was born and brought up in Thornhill, but he has travelled extensively throughout Scotland, fishing and shooting. He feels that the present policy of letting shooting by the day, rather than for the more normal five or six years, is bad for the hill. The temptation is for the guns to shoot into the stock, and that is the road to ruin, as far as a moor is concerned.

'One day last year we had an army of shooters, keepers, beaters and Land-Rovers here, and they shot five grouse between them.'

Keepers and gillies rely on the tips they receive from their gentlemen to make up their income. One day Andrew was asked to load for Lord Hailsham. He was not looking forward to the experience, for he was sure that they would have little in common and not much to say all day.

Lord Hailsham was sporting an old, worn game-bag, and, to break the ice, Andrew commented, 'You'll be needing a new game-bag soon, My Lord.'

'Oh', came the reply, 'I couldn't afford that!'

Andrew thought to himself: 'Well, there'll be no much in this old bugger for me at the end of the week!'

However, as the days progressed, Andrew found Lord Hailsham to be as fine a companion as he could wish for— delighted to talk about everyday things and as sociable as could be. But he declined to tell me what 'the old bugger' came up with at the end of the week!

He once took Audrey Hepburn, the film star, salmon-fishing and chose the Otter Pool as being the best chance. Ms Hepburn looked down to the jumble of rocks and exclaimed, 'I can't get down to that disgusting place!' So Andrew had to half-carry his lady to the water's edge.

'Unless you can Spey cast, you're not going to do much damage on some of the top beats because of the steep sides. I used to spend half my day climbing trees to retrieve flies. But one of the finest casters I ever had the pleasure of fishing with was Jackie Charlton, the footballer. Now there was a man who knew how to use a salmon rod!'

Andrew thinks the Nith is a far better sea-trout water than a salmon river. The lower beat has six pools, but the best pools are all on Nith Linns. A powerful rod is needed to stop the fish running out of the pools, because the steep banks make it impossible to follow them for any distance.

Poaching is a constant problem on the Nith because the main road follows the river closely for much of its length. Andrew remembers one day watching nine pairs of salmon on the redds in a little tributary. Next morning, not a fish was to be seen. However, footmarks were visible on the river bank, so he followed them, all the way to the estate boundary and on to the next moor. There, in a gully on the hill, were two sacks of salmon.

Andrew hurried home for the Land-Rover, but by the time he was back on the hill, sack and salmon had gone. The only way the fish could have been removed was by vehicle or pony. No tyre marks were visible on the hill, but grazing peacefully nearby was a shepherd's pony, and Andrew could clearly see hoof-prints close to where the salmon had lain. So he went on until he came to the shepherd's house and asked him, 'Is that your pony in the field, John?'

'Aye', said John.

'And are you the only one that uses it?'

'Aye', came the answer again.

'Well', said Andrew. 'It's a funny thing, but there were two sacks of salmon on the hill this afternoon, and now they've both gone.'

The shepherd admitted that he had loaned the pony to two men to carry the salmon away, and that they had been bound for Muirkirk. Four hours later, complete with policeman and search warrant, Andrew caught the poachers as they cleaned the salmon, carefully putting aside the roe for use as bait. They were fined £250 each, but refused to say to whom they proposed to sell the fish.

Andrew once considered leaving the estate when he was offered a job with the Earl of Stair.

'There was a palace of a house, but the wages were low and you had to trap and sell rabbits to make ends meet. Not for me!'

But many a night Andrew would return home and tell

his wife to pack their bags and get ready to leave. For if you were 'wrong with the Duke in the morning, then you were wrong all day'. If the line was ragged on the hill, the Duke would shout and roar at all and sundry until it was as he wanted it.

Indeed, Andrew remembers the Duke of Marlborough at a pheasant shoot getting hell from the Laird for daring to leave his appointed position. More often than not, however, the phone would ring in the evening:

'Hunter, I hope you haven't thought too much about what was said at the butts today?'

'No, My Lord, I've forgotten about it all', Andrew would reply, and that was an end to the matter.

I was to spend the night in Glasgow, so after leaving Andrew Hunter, I drove north up the A76, over fair Kirkconnel Lea and past De'il's Dyke. Like most Scots, I am a great admirer of Robert Burns, and as I travelled, every signpost roused thoughts of the great man.

Strange to relate, there is no record of Robert Burns ever going fishing; perhaps he was always too busy with his other much-loved sport, the lassies, to find time to fish. Certainly, he pursued his interest in the lassies with as much vigour and determination as any angler in pursuit of fish. He had fourteen known children, nearly half of them born out of wedlock.

Burns described the pleasures of the fair sex as 'The first of human joys, our chiefest pleasure here below.' If only he had discovered the second, fishing, then he might have found greater comfort and contentment in his short, turbulent life.

I stopped in the small village of Mauchline, and as I walked into Poosey Nancy's, near the bridge, thoughts of another man came flooding back. Many years ago a good friend of mine, Tony Sykes, rented fishing on the River Ayr at Mauchline. I was invited to try the water, but after a hard, fruitless, cold day, I began to despair of ever seeing a salmon, let alone catching one. So saying to my companion, I announced that enough was enough, and stamped off to the comfort of the pub. Imagine my exasperation when, as I was barely half-way down my first pint, in walked Tony carrying a beautiful fresh-run salmon of about 8 lb.

'Told you to persevere, didn't I? You've only yourself to blame. No staying power, you Edinburgh folk, that's your trouble.'

Ten years were to pass before the truth was out. Tony was as cold and tired as I was, but out of sheer determination he decided to have one last cast. He quickly packed up and followed me pub-wards. On the way he met two small boys, who just happened to have a salmon. In no time at all a deal had been struck, money had changed hands, and my discomfiture ensured. But for ten years I had to listen to Tony's account of what determination can do before he finally confessed.

My next call was to be on the recently retired head-keeper of the Linlithgow Estates, near Edinburgh, Willie Drysdale. I had already heard of Willie in the south-west, for he had been both companion and colleague to Walter Maxwell and Andrew Hunter at Thornhill before moving to Linlithgow and becoming one of Scotland's senior gentlemen's gentlemen.

Nor was I any stranger to Hopetoun. As a Boy Scout in Edinburgh, my favourite weekend camping site was in the woods near White Quarry and Midhope. Near to the old Dove Cot is a little bridge, and in the pool below the bridge, an outfall pipe where trout gathered. After our evening meal I would walk up from camp with a piece of string and a bent pin and, after carefully tying a strand of red or blue cotton to the pin, lie on the concrete cover of the pipe trying to persuade trout to commit suicide. I never caught one, but I had endless pleasure watching them rise and dash at the lure.

It so happens that Willie Drysdale is father-in-law of Jim Seaton, Features Editor of *The Scotsman*, to which I have contributed a number of articles over the years. Jim drove with me to meet Willie Drysdale at his cottage near Queensferry.

Willie is a wry sparrow of a man—keen-eyed, humorous and alert. He does not allow advancing years to hinder his pleasure in sport, and last season, in a blizzard, he had two spring salmon from the Tummel: 'They went 9 lb and 17 lb—not bad for an old man!'

pleasure in sport, and last season, in a blizzard, he had two spring salmon from the Tummel: 'They went 9 lb and 17 lb—not bad for an old man!'

Willie was born and brought up in the Lowther Hills and worked on Bowhill, North Sanquhar and Drumlanrig. He did a lot of fishing as a lad, since there wasn't much else to do in the country; 'In spite of what Robert Burns said!' He used a hazel branch as a rod, a line of red hemp, a bait hook and worm. He had no reel. But he caught plenty of trout, and grayling, too.

Willie remembers Nith and Annan as great rivers, always full of fish with 35/40 lb grey-backs caught regularly each autumn. Indeed, salmon were so plentiful that folk hardly bothered to fish for sea-trout.

The school was run by local farmers, known as the Board. They would descend during the season and take a dozen laddies to help with farm work—turnip-thinning or tattie-lifting. Down would go the slates and the boys would storm off, happy for any excuse to be out of school.

This was during the First World War, when, compared to most of the population, farmers were pretty well off. Some took their corn to the local mill to have it ground for white bread, but most country folk ate black bread.

School dinners were unknown in those days, and Willie's mother used to bake scones for him to take to school. Six or seven lads, in a bunch, would go off over the hills to school, five miles there and five miles back, regardless of the weather.

Willie left school when he was thirteen. It was July. In

August he was on the hill, working on the Cowhill Estate for the princely sum of fifteen shillings a week: 'I thought I was a king!'

After four-and-a-half years, his wages were raised to £1 per week, and after a further year he moved to a neighbouring estate for thirty-five shillings, then the top wage for an agricultural worker. Keepers were also provided with a suit of clothes and for special days, when the great folk came, a kilt.

Willie remembers that on these occasions the head-keeper would line everyone up and slowly inspect them to make sure they were properly turned out. Few were not, for jobs were hard to come by in those days. But Willie didn't like the kilt.

'I hated that damned kilt. On a frosty morning, wading through wet turnips, the backs of your legs would be all chapped and raw.'

Nobody trained Willie Drysdale. He learned from the old keepers. Even as a boy he was out with them on Saturdays, setting traps, or on the river, or helping the shepherds with lambing or hay-making.

Estates could afford to employ a number of keepers in those days. The position is very different today, and keepers have to be able to turn their hands to every aspect of sporting and agricultural work.

Willie reared between 12,000 and 15,000 pheasants each year. About 4,000 were kept for the estate and the remainder were sold to neighbouring landowners. Willie had no ready-mixed food for his pheasants in those days. It all had to be laboriously prepared by hand: grease, ground meat, minced rabbit, eggs, rice, all boiled up with milk, then dried and mixed again with barley meal. It was a long, tedious job. Broody hens were each given a clutch of young birds and a man stood by all day with a gun to ward off the crows, jackdaws and hawks.

The first indication of trouble was generally the sound the birds make when danger threatens: 'You'd hear an old cock bird, swearing away, or a blackbird going. Then you'd know a fox or stoat was in. But when all the birds were singing and happy, it was a grand sound. And the young birds soon learned the danger sounds. When a hawk came winging over, the old hen would gie a bit chirrl and the wee birds would crouch to the ground.'

Willie was fond of his charges and went to endless trouble to keep them safe and prepare them properly for their short lives on release. One of the most disturbing aspects of a day's shoot was when it was over and he had to go round the woods, looking for winged birds.

'That was always a bad time, after all the time and trouble you'd taken rearing them. I've seen hundreds of birds shot in a day, 800 once to six double guns. I needed a cart to bring them all home. Next day I went round the woods and picked up more than 50 wounded birds.'

I asked Willie if the reason for so many wounded birds was the poor marksmanship of the gentlemen. He smiled and told me of the worst shot he had ever seen.

'Roy Rogers came here once, you know. He left his horse, Trigger, in Edinburgh and came out with the late Willie Merrilee, who used to be Chief Constable. Now Roy Rogers may have been the "cat's pyjamas" with a six-shooter in Texas, but, believe me, he couldn't hit a barn door with a twelve-bore at Hopetoun! I've never seen such a useless hand with a gun in all my life!'

When Willie Drysdale came from Dumfriesshire to Hopetoun, he found it difficult to get used to all the people. His Lowther Hills, where he could walk all day without meeting another soul, seemed very distant, and he often found himself longing for their peace and quiet. But the Lothian folk were friendly, and the Drysdales soon settled in.

Lots of shale mines and shallow workings extended under the estate, and one morning Willie was setting snares for rabbits in the woods when he heard a voice behind him.

'Well, keeper, whit are you doing the day?'

Willie looked round and found a dozen men, black with dust, sitting eating their lunch under a tree.

'Where the devil did you lot come from?'

'Oh, keeper, you'll ha' a bit to go before you catch us!'

'How did you get by me?'

'By you! We went under you! Look!'

Sure enough, they had come out of the mine through a small hole in the ground.

Willie had a bite and a yarn with them before they went back down. They told him that, in times past, herring were hung up on strings, using the glow from their phosphorescent bodies to light the mines and that the women used to carry out the coal, in baskets, on their heads. But it was dull, slatey coal and not very good on the fire.

These mines have all gone now, and the spoil heaps have been levelled. When I was a boy, the red shale heaps marred the landscape around Queensferry, and the little roads switchbacked with evidence of subsidence. Terrible stories were told of horses and carts disappearing into the bowels of the earth, driver and all, and I have always driven along these by-ways with extreme caution, expecting the worst at every corner.

Probably the worst part of any keeper's task is controlling poachers. Willie found it hard, unpleasant work.

'You can't stop it, no matter how hard you try, and it's a filthy job, especially for your poor wife. I'd go out at eleven o'clock at night and be in the woods until near dawn. I'd get back home covered in frost, aching in every limb. Sometimes, if I'd heard a whisper, I'd take a policeman along. Food was hard to come by in those days and many folk were desperate.

'If I'd been out all night, then I had some time off in the morning, but I was still expected back at work in the afternoon. No fancy favours either, such as overtime or pensions!

'We caught a lot of poachers, poor devils. You see, we

knew the woods like the backs of our hands, and we also knew exactly where the poachers would run. But we could run faster, head them off, and put them into the quarry or river. Then we'd have them.'

Willie always carried a big wooden batten, but he never hit anyone unless he was attacked first, '... and I've had some bashings in my time, I can tell you!'

Poachers are much worse today, since they have no need of the birds for food. All they want is some easy money. Willie has twice been threatened with a shotgun: 'Come you a step nearer, keeper, and I'll blow your bloody brains out!'

Willie complained that today a poacher will as soon stick a knife in a keeper's back or break his neck as look at him.

'In the old days, if they were caught, they came quietly and took their punishment. Many's the time I've turned a blind eye or had a word with the fellow rather than catch him in the woods. I knew full well what was going on, and how well or badly off these folk were.'

But Willie has a philosophical approach to the problem and accepts that, if you are going to be a keeper, then it is no use moaning. You either get on with it or get out.

When he was a keeper at Cloven Castle, in Ayrshire, Willie used to finish at 2 pm and then be out from 10.30 pm until 5.30 am, night after night after night. More often than not, he had neither sight nor sound of poachers, but Mrs Drysdale used to wait at home, never knowing whether Willie would come back in one piece or covered in bruises.

He gave one poacher a good scare. Willie noticed three men by the river. Two were after rabbits and the third was sniggering salmon. Willie crept up behind the fisher and gave a great shout. The man got such a fright that he jumped straight into the 12 ft deep pool.

'Help!' he screamed. 'Help! I canna swim!'

So Willie had to get in and pull him out. In spite of

Willie saving his life, the man still refused to say who his friends were. When the case came to court, the poacher got off for lack of evidence.

As a young man, Willie's life was very much controlled by the estate. No rules and regulations governed terms of employment, and no day was a recognised day off. It was seven days a week, and seven nights as well, just in case the Laird needed him. If Willie wanted a holiday, he could take it only when the head-keeper decided. In March, when the rabbit-killing had finished, the head-keeper might say: 'Now Willie, if you're wanting a day or two off, you'd better take them now. You'll not be getting them when the pheasant-rearing starts.'

A lot of folk make fun of keepers, saying that they have never been off the estate, let alone out of Scotland. But in the early years of this century, there was little chance of doing either. The head-keeper's word was law, and the Laird, 'Damn near God himself!'

Conditions have much improved over the years, and keepers now have many secured advantages in their employment: house, fuel, electricity and telephone. But, as so many gillies and keepers commented to me: 'It would be nice to be addressed by my Christian name, rather than surname. Oh, you get used to it, but it would be nice, sometimes, to be spoken to, rather than at.'

I asked Willie Drysdale if, given the choice, he would be a keeper again.

'Looking back', he said, 'I've had a good life and I've made a lot of good friends—Jimmy Gillon and MacHardy at Balmoral, Andrew Hunter and Walter Maxwell at Thornhill. And I have my health. Yes, I suppose I would choose to be a keeper again, if I'd the chance. But not this chasing and hounding of poachers, going out night after night. No, I wouldn't do that again, not for all the money in the world!'

Darkness was falling as we left Willie's cottage, and spring frost sparkled on bare trees. The sound of pheasants coughing in the wood followed us. Surely, I thought sadly, it was not too much to expect, to be called 'Willie', or 'Mr Drysdale', once in a while? I felt privileged to have had the chance to talk to Willie and to address him so. The memory of the hours I spent with him will warm many a long winter night.

CHAPTER 11

Forfarshire,
Ned Coates, David Hanton
and the South Esk

The South Esk is one of the finest salmon rivers in Scotland and Ned Coates has gillied there all his life. Ned, and his charming wife, Alison, run a small guest house close to the sea at St Cyrus, near Montrose, and as I parked my car, salt spray from a February storm bade me welcome.

Ned Coates is of medium height, stockily built, with a weather-beaten face and ready smile. Most of his life has been spent outdoors, and few days pass without he is at work on the river as gillie and mentor to gentlemen on the Kinnaird Beat.

Eleven salmon had been caught on the day I arrived, and Ned consulted his fishing book for details of the previous five days' catches: Monday, twenty; Tuesday, fourteen; Wednesday, three; Thursday, four; Friday, nine. Ned explained that the water was high on Wednesday and Thursday, otherwise more salmon would have been taken. Opening day on Kinnaird, 16 February, had produced seventeen fish.

Ned claims that anyone can catch salmon in spring, when 'They'll grab at anything.' While this has not always been my experience, it certainly seems true of the South Esk. Over the years Ned has often seen upwards of twenty salmon caught in a day.

Ned's father was head-keeper at Kinnaird, and both his brothers worked as gillies on the river: Jimmy, who served in the Airborne Division during the Second World War, died twelve years ago; David, wounded in Italy, retired recently. Ned served in the Royal Marines and after the war, in 1946, married Alison, the daughter of the Duke of Windsor's butler.

Ned has gillied for many notable sportsmen: Lord Strathmore, Lord Dalhousie, the Duke of Sutherland, the Hon. John Leslie, and Lord Strathesk. The Rileys, of motor-car fame, brought their children to the South Esk, and Ned's father taught them how to fish: 'When everything was good, the country was good and the river full of fish.'

The South Esk rises in Balmoral Forest, among the crags and corries of Lochnagar. Cairn Bannoch (3,314 ft), Fafernie (3,274 ft) and Broad Cairn (3,268 ft) hurry the stream down Glen Doll and Glen Clova, past Cortachy Castle, ancient stronghold of the Ogilvies. It gathers in Prosen Water at Inverquharity, and flows forty-nine miles through the Angus hills and farmlands to Montrose and the cold North Sea.

The name Montrose was made famous in Scottish history by James Graham, the first Marquess. Montrose took an active part in drawing up the National Covenant in 1637, but soon became disillusioned with the plotting and counter-plotting of Argyll, the Covenanters and Hamilton.

In spite of nine months' imprisonment in Edinburgh Castle, Montrose vowed, 'I will save the throne in Scotland or die.' After a series of brilliant victories, he was surprised at Philiphaugh on 13 September, 1645, by a Commonwealth force under the command of General David Leslie. The Royalist army was routed and Montrose fled to France.

But when Charles I was executed, James Graham returned to Scotland in a futile attempt to raise the Royal Standard on behalf of the murdered King's son. The ill-planned venture ended in defeat and disaster. Montrose was betrayed by the Assynt Macleods and held captive in their castle at Ardvrek. He was taken to Edinburgh, tied on the back of a small Highland pony, and there, on 21 May, 1650, hanged and dismembered as a traitor.

> *He is coming! He is coming!*
> *Like a bridegroom from his room,*
> *Came the hero from the prison,*
> *To the scaffold and the doom.*
> *There was glory on his forehead,*
> *There was lustre in his eye,*
> *And he never walked to battle*
> *More proudly than to die.*

Like the followers of Montrose, Ned wears the kilt.

'Two things I have never owned,' he told me, 'a wrist-watch and a pair of long trousers. Time goes by quickly enough without me watching, and I have worn the kilt all my days. A kilt is grand for work on the river.

'It gives great freedom of movement; and if a gentleman has difficulty bringing salmon in, I just wade out and get it. The kilt floats up around me and soon dries again.'

Ned gillied for his first gentlemen when he was only fifteen years old. His father set him to work with Sir

Eastman Bell and Sir Harold Gillies, the surgeon. Sir Harold used to paint, and young Ned had to carry easel, paints and brushes as well as fishing-tackle down to the river. In those days many gentlemen fished with silver and golden sprats and brought huge jars of them to the river. Sprats require constant attention and are awkward to attach to the hook. But they can be a deadly bait, particularly in spring, when fish lie deep in the pools.

Sir Eastman Bell smoked continually and stood, up to his waist in the freezing river, puffing away like a steam-engine at big, flat Turkish cigarettes. A salmon was hooked and after a great struggle Sir Eastman brought it to the side and told Ned to gaff it. Although his father had shown Ned how to use a gaff, and he had seen it demonstrated many times, he had never done it himself. The young lad became excited and jabbed away until he snapped the cast and the salmon was lost.

The irate angler roared at Ned: 'Incompetent young devil! Don't you know how to gaff a salmon? I shall speak to your father!' So when Ned got home that evening, he had another telling-off and went to bed supperless and miserable.

But Ned thinks he must have improved during the week, for when the gentlemen left they gave his mother £26.

'Or they might just have been sorry for being so angry with me', he said. 'Whatever it was, we were glad of the tip, for £26 was a lot of money then.'

Many anglers and gillies have mixed feelings about using sprats and prawns. Taking a prawn down a pool sometimes seems to scare every salmon for miles; at other times it instantly attracts fish. Ned's story reminded me of a tale told by Gordon Dagger, fishery-manager and head-gillie on the Forss River in Caithness. Gordon was fishing in Ireland a few years back and in spite of trying everything they could think of, he and his companion remained fishless.

Gordon determined to change flies and try again, but his partner declared that he would 'sort them out' with a prawn. He leapt into his car and drove to the nearest village, where he purchased a large bag of prawns. Gordon left him by the river, furiously hurling a prawn across the stream, completely confident that at any moment a salmon would grab it.

An hour later Gordon found his friend sitting by the pool, a dejected heap, still fishless and clutching an empty paper bag. The remains of prawns were scattered round.

'What happened?' enquired Gordon.

'The damned fish wouldn't eat them, so I ate them myself' came the disconsolate reply.

Apart from military service, Ned had been away from the river for only four years. He was persuaded by a gentleman to go to look after an estate in Essex. Ned described his employer, Mr Watts, as being 'A typical Scottish farmer, although he was English.'

It was a small estate with good low-ground shooting for pheasants and partridge, and while Ned managed the property, his wife, Alison, who is a superb cook, looked after the house. Each year Mr Watts used to visit the Outer Hebrides to fish on the 'heather isle', Lewis. Ned would drive north in a van with all the tackle to get things ready; Mr Watts and his guests flew up from London. They always stayed in the County Hotel in Stornoway, and their first week was spent on the River Creed, a mile south of the town.

The Creed is a classic sea-trout river, offering easy access for fish. It rises to the west of Stornoway, on the moor below Beinn Bhearnach, and flows east through Loch an Ois and Loch a'Chlachain, which are used to control water-levels in the river. It empties into the wide, sheltered bay that encloses Stornoway harbour, past tiny Greeta Island.

Sandy MacMasters was head-gillie on the Creed in those days, and most years saw between fifty and sixty sea-trout caught during the week. The remainder of the holiday was always spent at Grimersta, on the west coast, among some of the finest salmon-fishing in the world.

When Ned returned to Scotland it was to work as gamekeeper for one of the great characters of the area, Big Bill Robertson, farmer and potato-merchant extraordinary. Big Bill met Ned at Bridge of Dun Station.

'Noo, Ned, whit wages do you get?'

Ned told him, '£10 a week.'

'Well, I'll gie ye the same, with free milk, free tatties and a free house. Dinna call me Bill or Sir. Just call me Boss!'

Bill Robertson took Ned to see 'his' river, a good beat on the South Esk, and asked what might be done to make it produce some sort of income. Bill was no fisherman. When Ned replied that a lot of folk would be prepared to pay good money to fish it, his 'Laird' looked startled. 'Oh, God man,' he said, scratching his big ears, 'I'm no that hard up yet that I have to let my water.'

So when gentlemen wrote seeking permission to fish, they never knew what to offer in return, for Bill Robertson didn't want payment in money. Before long the gun-room in the big house was full to the ceiling with cases of whisky. One of the gentlemen, Mr Caird, from Dundee, had a fine suit made for Mr Robertson, but Bill liked nothing better than to wander down to the river at lunch-time and have a yarn and a dram with his guests.

'It's changed days now on the river', said Ned, 'and so are many of the gentlemen who come to fish. All that seems to matter is numbers of fish. They've little time for a blether, or anything else for that matter.'

Although Ned has spent most of his time salmon-fishing, he's 'never cast a trout rod in my life.' His father, as head-keeper at Kinnaird, was very much involved in stalking and shooting. The late Earl of Southesk was a keen sportsman and Ned showed me a copy of a page from the Earl's game-book giving details of 'notable' bags:

Forfarshire, Ned Coates, David Hanton and the South Esk

'Largest bags of game killed when I have been shooting.

Capercailzie	60	Fotheringham	51 twice at Kinnaird
Black game	92	Drumlanrig	All cocks
Grouse	1,887	Langholm	Self, 431; 121 at one drive
Pheasants	3,012	Fasque	Six guns
Pheasants	1,452	Fasque	J. Gladstone, Kintore, and self
Partridges	398	Cambridgeshire	Stetchworth
Snipe	194	Albania	W. S. Fothringham and self
Woodcock	48	Albania	Self
Woodpigeons	228	Crimonmogate	Self
Wild duck	315	Fasque	Six guns
Wild duck	309	Glendye	J. Gladstone and self
Hares	440	Lancashire	
Rabbits	2,010	Aberdeenshire	Keith Hall
Quail	300	Egypt	Two days over 300
Roe deer	28	Drumlanrig	
Wild duck	156	Albania	Dropped many more

'Woodpigeons—100 or over shot by self:

Dec	14,	1893,	131	Crimonmogate
Nov	20,	1895,	105	Crimonmogate
Aug	19,	1896,	105	Crimonmogate
Jan	20,	1897,	102	Crimonmogate
Sept	7,	1897,	124	Crimonmogate
Sept	9,	1897,	228	Crimonmogate (two hours)
Aug	17,	1899,	107	Crimonmogate
Aug	18,	1899,	103	Crimonmogate
Dec	17,	1900,	118	Crimonmogate
Sept	10,	1903,	109	Crimonmogate
Jan	3,	1917,	101	Kinnaird
Sept	22,	1933,	105	Crimonmogate

'Pheasants killed by self at one rise:

Nov	10,	1914,	305	Fasque
Nov	14,	1912,	272	Fasque
Nov	17,	1911,	321 and 281	Fasque
Dec	17,	1910,	201	Fasque
Nov	10,	1910,	311	Fasque

Nov	11,	1909,	172	Fasque
Nov	7,	1908,	231	Fasque
Nov	16,	1906,	206	Fasque
Nov	7,	1900,	600	Fasque
Dec	13,	1896,	228	Fasque (238 shots) Hendrie
Nov	26,	1889,	103	Fasque (107 shots)
Nov	28,	1889,	98	Fasque (101 shots)

'Score of 600 was taken by E. Balfour and two keepers.
The Hendrie rise was taken by Lady Lewis and two others and took under 17 minutes.

'48 grouse with 48 shots; one miss; two with one shot.
63 partridges with 63 shots.
79 pheasants with 79 shots.'

I read the page in silence and astonishment. Clearly the Earl of Southesk was a remarkable and dedicated shot, and bad news for birds from Aberdeenshire to Albania.

I stayed at St Cyrus with Ned and Alison, listening long into the night to his stories, the sound of the storm loud against the windows. The following morning, sunlight sparkled on the sea and I visualised the Esk salmon, bars of spring silver, surging through the surf, heading for Montrose, where Ned Coates would be waiting to greet them.

I drove inland from Montrose, going by way of the ancient market town of Forfar, and then by Kirriemuir, towards Cortachy and the Braes of Angus. Here, more than sixty peaks rise to more than 2,000 ft, and the long glens of Isla, Prosen, Clova, Ogil, Lethnot and Esk cut deeply into the wild hills. Lochs Brandy, Wharral, Lee and Muick nestle among the crags. It is a magnificent, beautiful, exciting land.

My elder brother and his family live in Kirriemuir, and it was through the kindness of their friend, David Laird, the Airlie Estate factor, that I had been given an introduction to the recently-retired head-keeper, David Hanton, and permission to fish Loch Brandy.

Loch Brandy does not contain large trout. It is not

stocked. It has no boats, and a basket of half-a-dozen, half-pound fish taken off the bank counts as a good catch. But it is one of the most beautiful lochs I have ever fished. If you are looking for a day out, really away from it all, then drive north from Thrums, J. M. Barrie's name for the ancient Burgh of Kirriemuir, on the B955, and you will not be disappointed. My own visit, with my family, was an eventful one, but that is another story ...

The following morning I headed back up the glen. This is Ogilvy country. In 1432 Sir Wallace Ogilvy, treasurer of Scotland, was granted permission by James I to fortify his tower of Eroly, the site of the present-day castle of Airlie.

The original structure was destroyed by that arch-schemer, Lord Lorne, Marquess of Argyll. It is said that, in his fury against the Ogilvies, the Marquess himself helped to tear down the castle. Perhaps he should have spared himself the effort, for, after nearly a quarter of a century variously supporting both Covenanter and Royalist, he was found guilty of treason and beheaded in Edinburgh on 27 May, 1661.

Nowadays, things are more peaceful in the land of the 'rapids of the river', Lintrathen. The rapids in question are the famous Reekie Linn, on the River Isla. Close to Bridge of Craigisla, the river is forced through a narrow wooded gorge. The water rushes over a great waterfall and spray hangs like smoke over the whirlpool and cavern of the Black Dubh. A mile or so further downstream is the equally impressive race and waterfall of Slug of Auchrannie.

The Romans knew this country. For several hundred years they struggled, and failed, to control the war-like tribes. At Battledykes, to the north-west of Forfar, is the site of a Roman fort large enough to have accommodated 26,000 soldiers.

As I crossed the Lemno Burn, the mist began to rise from the crest of Hill of Finavon, and I could almost see those long-gone legionaries cursing over the heather, thinking of Mediterranean sun and their far-off homes.

The home I was making for stood in the well-ordered calm of Cortachy Castle Estate, close to where the waters of Prosen join the South Esk, and the man I had come to see was David Hanton. I opened the garden gate and walked up the short path, through a neat, well-kept garden to the front-door of the sandstone cottage.

David welcomed me warmly and took me through to the sitting-room. A man of medium height, stocky and well set up, he had a twinkle in his eyes and a bright, ready smile.

'Do you know, when I was seventeen, in 1915, I joined the Gordon Highlanders and I can remember it as clearly as though it were yesterday. Now, last week I put away two spools of nylon and I've completely forgotten where I laid them. How do you account for that?'

'If it's anything like my house, David, someone has just "borrowed" them or tidied away. All one can do is wait and hope!'

The Hanton family has been on the estate for many years. David's grandfather, Willie Hamilton senior, was head-keeper for nearly sixty years. Two of his sons were in service, and his own father was also head-keeper. David told me that he had worked on the estate all his life.

'But, you know, it was a close-run thing. I was badly wounded during the second Battle of the Marne. We'd been ordered to take a crest called Vimy Ridge, and I was a bomber, running about with a sack of Mills bombs on my back. Daft it was! Well, I was in a vineyard when I was hit by a "whiz-bang", a 14 lb shell, and it took half my calf off. It was like being hit by the side of a house. As I fell to the ground I remember thinking, "Well, that's the end of your keepering days, my lad!" But I recovered, after sixteen months in a hospital in Yorkshire, and I've been a keeper ever since.

'I was brought up among dogs and snares and traps and fishing. When I was about five-years-old I was sent up to my grandfather at Rottal, in Glen Clova, to recover from an illness. What a grand place for a young lad! There was a little burn in front of the lodge, the Burn of Heughs, which came down from Ben Tirran. It had fine pools and a trout under every stone.

'I'd put a worm on a bit of string and a stick and I soon had them out. I thought it was paradise, and was always away down to the river to fish. I sent a postcard home to tell them how I was getting on and what I was doing, and I remember having the greatest difficulty in spelling the word "trout". Five times I wrote it, and five times it had to be rubbed out before I got it right. But that's where I got the fishing fever, and it's stayed with me ever since.'

Like most country lads, David loved trout fishing.

'I never had much time for salmon-fishing then, and just liked to puddle along the edges for trout and parr. Full well I knew that we weren't supposed to take parr, but it was a great temptation and hard to resist.

'One morning I was fishing away, my pockets full of parr, when who should I see but Jock Murray, the water-bailiff, coming towards me. He was a pretty tough customer and not to be trifled with. We youngsters were all afraid of him.

' "How are you getting on, loon?" he said.

' "Oh, nothing much doing, Mr Murray. Very quiet!"

' "Is your father fishing the day?"

' "Aye, he's down at the pool."

'I saw Jock walk off and hide himself in the trees overlooking the pool where father was fishing. In these days, if you got a well-mended kelt, then you might not be above taking him home. For all the pay you got, and with a family to feed, times were hard and a salmon would provide a meal.

'I prayed that father wouldn't catch a kelt with Jock Murray standing watching. After what seemed an age, he moved off, but to this day I can feel the fear in my throat.

'There were a lot of staff up at the big house in those

days: butler, footmen, housemaids, nursery staff, three lassies in the pantry, three or four laundry-maids, four in the kitchen, cook, scullery-maid, coachmen, grooms. It needed a special train to bring them all up from England!

'There was an empty stall or two in the stables, so I used to feed and water the dogs and have them ready in the morning, before the gentlemen went off shooting. All the tips were in golden sovereigns then—well, most of them. One gentleman, a great big fellow, or so he seemed to a lad, had a huge bag of cartridges. You'd have thought he was going off to fight the war all by himself!

'I had to carry this bag around all day, with him blasting away non-stop at big fat hares and partridge—any amount of them, and all slung across to me to carry. It was hard, heavy work, and at the end of the day he gave me a two-shilling tip! They were hard times, I can tell you!

'Most of the gentlemen came to shoot. Not many were interested in the fishing. The odd one or two would spend their time at the river, and some were very good at it, too. If it was a bad day for the hill, then the shooters might go down to the river.

'I remember one gentleman, no hand at all with the rod, coming back with a good fish of 12 lb. It was laid out on the table with a label attached, addressed to the only gentleman in the party who was a real fisher. Next morning there was a 17 lb fish lying there, addressed to the shooter!

'The biggest salmon I ever caught here was a fine fish of 23 lb. Got him in heavy water, after a spate, and what a fight he put up! But there aren't the same numbers of salmon in the river now. Where there's one now, there were ten before, and we always have to keep a good eye open for the poachers.

'The worst time here for poachers was at the end of petrol rationing, after the last war. We had organised gangs coming from as far away as Airdrie to steal fish.

'Ralph Hunter was a gillie here for many years, and an expert salmon-fisher. He just couldn't abide the poachers and waged constant war on them. One night he got wind of a gang on the river and organised himself and his wife to trap them.

' "Away you go with the car, and I'll go up the river bank and we'll meet at the bridge."

'So off went Mrs Hunter. But the police had the same idea and were blocking the road and wouldn't let her past. But she was a determined lady, and if her husband had asked her to meet him on the bridge, then that's exactly what she was going to do.

'Nothing the policeman could say would stop her, and in the end she just drove straight through the road-block, running over the policeman's foot in the process, leaving him hopping about the centre of the road mad with rage.

' "You know that bobbie, Beattie?" she said. "He's just stupid. Tried to stop me when I was only doing what Ralph asked."

'It was the policeman's fault that he was run over, not her's!

'Another night all the dogs began barking and yelping, so Ralph pulled on his trousers and went out on to the bridge. There were the poachers, bold as brass, gassing the river and taking salmon out by the dozen.

'Ralph dashed back to his long-suffering wife: "Telephone every policeman in the county. I'll try and stop them!"

'When the police and the Fishery Board people got to the scene, the poachers had long since gone, giving Ralph a good bashing before leaving. So everyone set off in hot pursuit. When I arrived on the river-bank, there was Ralph, still shaken, looking down at more than 200 salmon.

' "There's some good ones there, Ralph", I said.

' "Aye, David, right enough. Let's be quick about it and have something for our trouble before they come back and count the things. It's about all the thanks we'll be getting!"

'We gillies are used to dealing with strange situations

and difficult individuals. It's all part of the job. Most of my gentlemen were considerate fellows and easy to please; and many were my good friends and fishing companions for years. But there were always one or two who took some handling.

'I remember once having a 'phone call from a neighbour and being asked to take a gentleman out for some sport with the sea-trout later in the evening. When I arrived at the river, it was four they were, not one at all.

'It's difficult enough with one angler, but four in the dark was about beyond me. I got them all set up, rods properly fitted together, reels, lines and casts all in order, gave them some basic instruction and spaced them out along the bank.

'By the time I'd finished setting the fourth gentleman off, the first was calling for help, saying his flies were all in a heap. Then the second gentleman got caught up in the trees, and I had to climb up and loose the flies. By that time the third one had managed to fall head-over-heels into the river, and the fourth was firmly hooked into a poor cow!

'I was rushing backwards and forwards from disaster to disaster, emptying waders, unfankling casts, tying new ones, extracting flies from trees and the backsides of humans and animals until I was exhausted.

'It was only then that I realised that since it was quite dark, they could hardly see the river, let along whether or not there were any flies on their casts or barbs on their flies. So I just sat in a corner and left them all to it!

'Do you know, at the end of the evening, they all said that it was one of the most enjoyable nights they'd ever had, and wasn't it just a pity they were leaving the following morning? Otherwise, they would have loved another "go". I was delighted to see them so happy, and even more delighted to see them go!

'There was another family used to come here, very fine folk and a pleasure to be with, the gentleman, his wife and three sons. One of the boys was a great cricketer and used to play with the Free Foresters. Now they hadn't much of an idea about fishing, but they were all keen to try, so I offered to give a bit help and instruction, should they want it.

'Well, one of the lads got set up and off he went, down the river, using the rod as though it were a huge whip, lashing and splashing away like a madman.

' "If you could perhaps manage to land your fly on the water just a little bit more lightly, then we might have the chance of a fish", I said. "Try to throw the line above the surface, not on to it. Let the line straighten out in mid-air. All you're doing just now is scaring them to death, and me, too, standing next to you!"

' "Well, let's see if you can do any better. Take the rod and show us how it's done!"

'I put up a size ten Shrimp Fly. Second cast, out he comes from behind his stone and grabs it! Well, they all got up from the river-bank and made a rush for the fish, and I had the devil of a job keeping them back until I'd tailed it!

' "There, as fine a salmon as you could ever wish to see. That's how it's done!"

' "No it isn't", said the lad. "I had them all pretty well stunned before you started!"

'The day before they were due to leave, they asked me if there might be the chance of a salmon to take home with them. But their beat was in poor condition, with little chance of a fish.

'Now I knew exactly where to find a fish, a few pools down, on another beat. So I arranged to meet them by their fishing-hut at six o'clock and told them not to start fishing until I arrived.

'Away I went, down the river to where it rushes round a promontory into fast, deep, white water. On the edge of the flow I hooked him and soon had him on the bank—a good, fresh-run fish of about 14 lb.

'I walked quietly upstream to the fishing-hut. There they all were, chattering away, watching the pool and wondering if they were going to get a fish. I came sneaking up behind, in the gloaming, and when they heard me on the gravel they all turned and asked if they should start fishing.

' "You may start as soon as you like now, for if you don't catch anything, there'll still be a fine fish for you to take home anyway!"

'And delighted they were to get it, as I'll be should I ever find my lost nylon again!'

'David, those are grand tales. Thank you for telling me them', I said.

'It would be a sad world if there was no one prepared to listen. I regard every season as though it might be my last. But there's a good many more salmon I have to catch before I take down my rod for the last time.'

I thanked David and Mrs Hanton and took my leave. Collecting the family, back in Kirriemuir, I headed north on the five-hour drive to Caithness. With David's stories and the memory of his gentle courtesy and humour, the time passed as easily and pleasantly as a summer shower.

Epilogue

Two thousand miles: driving, listening, talking, recording, writing. Homely cottages, warm firesides, courteous people: laughter mixed with bitter-sweet memories. Strong, wind-burned, kindly faces: humour and wisdom gathered from years on hill, moor and river.

These are the *real* gentlemen, the keepers, stalkers, and gillies: men who have spent a lifetime caring for their stags, salmon, grouse and game; who have devoted all their energies to providing their guests with sport and pleasure.

My strongest impression is one of admiration for the vast knowledge they have of their sport; my strongest feeling, one of disappointment at the ill-usage they so often receive at the hands of their 'gentlemen'.

Without exception, these men deplore the destruction being meted out to Atlantic salmon stocks through over-fishing at sea and in the estuaries. Viewing the present situation against a background of more than sixty years' day-to-day experience, they presage with one accord the passing of the 'good old days', when each morning brought the chance of a few fish, or maybe more.

They have presided helplessly over the demise of one of the world's great sporting fish, while their 'gentlemen' stood idly by, allowing it to happen. It is little wonder that many of my gillies were bitter and not too sorry to hang up their rods and be done with it.

Yes, times change, and the fortunes and conditions of employment of present-day keepers have vastly improved. But it is still a completely demanding, twenty-four hour job, and the modern keeper is just as much at the beck and call of his master as ever a keeper was before.

As to the 'gentlemen', they are more demanding than ever. Having paid dearly to obtain even second-rate fishing or shooting, they expect value for money, and at times they are not over particular about the methods they use to achieve it.

I suppose that is the nature of the beast, but it seems to me that fishing and shooting are becoming more and more professional and commercialised. Much of the simple pleasure of being out on hill or loch, like a lightly hooked salmon, have gone forever.

I hope that I have managed to capture a small part of the 'old days' between the covers of this book, and I make no apology for my criticism of present attitudes. My views are shared by the gillies and keepers I met, and I could wish for no finer company than these honourable, sporting gentlemen's gentlemen.